Superintendent Case Studies

Other Books by Wafa Hozien

Effective Superintendent Decision-Making Practices

Elementary School Principals in Action: Resolving Case Studies in Leadership

Improving Instructional Practice: Resolving Issues in Leadership through Case Studies

Reflective Practice: Case Studies for High School Principals

SLLA Crash Course: Approaches for Success

Superintendent Case Studies

Creating Meaningful Engagement

Wafa Hozien

ROWMAN & LITTLEFIELD
Lanham • Boulder • New York • London

Published in partnership with the American Association of School Administrators
Published by Rowman & Littlefield

An imprint of The Rowman & Littlefield Publishing Group, Inc.
4501 Forbes Boulevard, Suite 200, Lanham, Maryland 20706
www.rowman.com

6 Tinworth Street, London SE11 5AL, United Kingdom

British Library Cataloguing in Publication Information Available

Library of Congress Cataloging-in-Publication Data
Names: Hozien, Wafa, author.
Title: Superintendent case studies : creating meaningful engagement / Wafa Hozien.
Description: Lanham : Rowman & Littlefield, [2019] | Includes bibliographical
   references.
Identifiers: LCCN 2018051089 (print) | LCCN 2019005541 (ebook) |
   ISBN 9781475848984 (Electronic) | ISBN 9781475848960 (cloth : alk. paper) |
   ISBN 9781475848977 (pbk. : alk. paper)
Subjects: LCSH: School superintendents—United States—Case studies. |
   School superintendents—Training of—Case studies. | School management and
   organization—United States—Case studies. | Educational leadership—Case studies.
Classification: LCC LB2831.72 (ebook) | LCC LB2831.72 .H39 2019 (print) |
   DDC 371.2/011—dc23
LC record available at https://lccn.loc.gov/2018051089

♾️™ The paper used in this publication meets the minimum requirements of American National Standard for Information Sciences—Permanence of Paper for Printed Library Materials, ANSI/NISO Z39.48–1992.

Printed in the United States of America

I dedicate this book to my brother Abdulmajeed Hozien, who has been there for me, always. This book is dedicated to that one person in your life, when you look up, he is around to lift you up.
Thank you Abdulmajeed.

For Muhammad, who challenges my thinking and whom I have a great deal of respect for;

For Nidal, who keeps me understanding and strengthens me.

Contents

SECTION II SUPPORTIVE SCHOOL COMMUNITY   71

Foreword

Dr. Wafa Hozien brings over 20 years of experience in education and leadership to her latest book. As the author of several books, her current series focusing on case studies aligned to the Professional Standards of Educational Leaders (PSEL) standards has the power to change the dialogue occurring in today's schools. Released in 2015 and adopted by many states, including Delaware, this latest iteration of standards for educational leaders recognizes the breadth and depth of the challenges facing today's administrators.

It is with urgency that today's school leaders must strive for excellence in meeting the ever-increasing demands being placed on them by all stakeholders – parents, community members, politicians, and most-importantly students. It's a new day in education as states implement new plans under the Every Student Succeeds Act (ESSA). Accountability remains high with rigorous standards for students, report cards for schools, and new vocabulary being added daily to their repertoire—trauma-informed practices, personalized learning, cultural responsiveness, grit, and the list continues. Pair this with the challenges that have always faced education—teacher shortages, not enough time for professional learning, and inadequate budgets. With so many challenges facing leaders, it's more important than ever to have standards that leaders can aspire to with the goal of ultimately increase outcomes for each student.

PSEL Standards truly run the gamut—having a mission and vision statement with core values that align to a school improvement plan; ensuring that professional norms and ethics are systemized to set high expectations for the entire learning community; creating a culture of shared leadership by building the capacity of school personnel and systematically involving the community in all aspects of the school. These standards reflect what we always knew – we can't do it alone! For the first time, ensuring equity and being culturally responsive are requirements so that leaders are creating opportunities for ALL students. Yes – curriculum, instruction, and assessment remain a priority, but for the first time creating a community of care and support for students is seen as an integral and necessary role for the school community. Operations and management are still an essential element of the work for any administrator, but the evolution of the role from manager to leader is reflected in the standards.

The challenges facing leaders are great, but the opportunities provided through these standards is greater. PSEL clearly articulates the role of a school leader at all levels of the organization. What are next steps? In one word – alignment. PSEL standards are the roadmap for reforming the work of school leaders. Alignment begins prior to employment which means leadership preparation programs should align to the precursor of PSEL – National Educational Leadership Preparation (NELP). Recently released, NELP, defines the performance expectations for a novice leader. With preparation programs aligned to NELP, licensure requirements for states must follow – ensuring that future leaders were given the opportunity to engage in coursework and experiences that would help them enter into a leadership role. With preparation programs aligned, schools have the responsibility of aligning selection and hiring practices to NELP and PSEL. Are hiring practices assessing mastery of skills across the standards or simply comprised of traditional interview questions and tasks?

Delaware is making great strides in the alignment of mentoring and induction programs for new leaders to PSEL standards. Aligning an induction program to PSEL that is led by successful practitioners, while providing 1:1 mentoring, is a promising practice for the state. Another essential element of a PSEL aligned system is evaluation. A daunting task for a state or local agency to undertake, but critical to the commitment of continuous learning and feedback. An evaluation system can methodically increase goal setting, reflection, and initiate honest dialogue. With preparation programs aligned, licensure requirements adjusted, hiring practices revisited, induction and mentoring to support our novice leaders, and an evaluation system that is measuring progress, only one thing remains—professional learning that is targeted, engaging, and intentionally aligned to PSEL.

The process of alignment seems completely feasible, but like standards that have come before them, PSEL sit on shelves in binders across the country as we race to put out the next perceived fire. Through Dr. Hozien's book we move the standards from the bookshelf to the conference table and, finally, to daily practice. Recognizing the urgency to align the everyday work of administrators to standards, from her research in the field of education leadership, Dr. Hozien has compiled numerous case studies and organized them around the 10 PSEL Standards. The case studies are relevant to today's leader and organized in an easy to facilitate format.

As a state education agency leader focused on school leaders, I have witnessed the power of conversation when using Dr. Hozien's case studies with current practitioners. I have used the case studies with mentors, novice leaders, and experienced leaders alike. In all of these circles, ideas were challenged, practices were validated, and knowledge was extended. Through the case studies, leaders simulate experiences through many lenses, so when faced with a similar situation in their day-to-day work, they'll be prepared to make thoughtful, sound decisions. With a direct alignment to PSEL, leaders are unpacking the standards in a meaningful and engaging manner.

Some of the districts in Delaware focus on a standard a month, others take a slower approach. Rolling out the standards won't be perfect—raising expectations and accountability across an organization is never easy. But start today, and use Dr. Hozien's book as a launching pad for this important work.

—Michael L. Saylor

Michael L. Saylor, Ph.D., School Leadership, Delaware Department of Education A former teacher, administrator, and national consultant, Michael currently leads school leadership initiatives for the Delaware Department of Education focusing on recruitment, retention, and professional learning. He recently led the state through an alignment of the administrator evaluation system to PSEL and launched a statewide mentoring and induction program.

Introduction

Our schools are multifaceted organizations that are constantly changing. Thus, new challenges continue emerging for school superintendents, who are now aware of the need to make a definite turn from traditional forms of school management to a new pedagogical approach to teaching, learning, and improving students' academic performance. School administrators are always innovating to meet the needs of their student populations, including the creation of community or full-service schools, thereby recognizing the need for public schools to prepare the whole child regardless of circumstances. With educational reforms, it is not enough to overcome these challenges by creating one solution for all issues across the board. It is essential to make an ethical commitment to address them alongside stakeholders involved in the teaching and learning processes and the dilemmas that result on a daily basis in our schools.

With this purpose in mind this book aims to train and empower school leaders to confront challenges in their institutions, acknowledging their role as eminently pedagogical. This book seeks to contribute to the training of future educational leaders through a number of cases and presenting a series of dilemmas. The main purpose of the cases is to foster reflection on these dilemmas among school leaders and other stakeholders and engage them in dialogue about potential solutions to those issues, giving them tools to confront similar situations at their schools.

Reflecting everyday experiences at schools around the country, this book presents a series of situations to be analyzed, compared, contrasted, studied, and discussed by those who want to be part of this new approach to education and school leadership. This book aims to encourage and contribute to the reflection on the situations that school administrators, along with their teams, must confront and resolve in their roles as pedagogical leaders. Therefore, it is intended for future educational leaders to take charge in transforming their schools into institutions of educational excellence.

For ease of use, this book has been developed with the practitioner in mind. It is designed to allow school administrators to take time to process and engage in critical-thinking activities that ensure that the school community is recognized with a deeper level of understanding. The core tenet here is that the school administrator shapes the educational programs of the school district, thereby making an effort to involve the school community toward school improvement. This is the central principle of this book.

Education plays a key role in determining how one spends one's adult life; a higher level of education means higher earnings, better health, and a longer life. By the same token, the long-term social and financial costs of educational failure are high. Those without the skills to participate socially and economically generate higher costs for health, income support, child welfare, and social security systems. So a fair and inclusive system that makes the advantages of education available to all is one of the most powerful levers to make society more equitable. Therefore, the intention of the author is that this book engages school administrators in conversations that lead to improving equity in education with three facets in mind: designing educational system, the practice as the head of a school district, and the resources available to them as school district leaders.

The book is divided into two sections. Section one is about issues of educational equity: recognizing the importance of educational equity as a measure of achievement, fairness, and opportunity in education. The study of education equity is often linked with that of excellence and equity. Educational equity depends on two main factors. The first is fairness, which implies that factors specific to the student's personal conditions should not interfere with the potential of academic success. The second important factor is inclusion, which refers to a comprehensive standard that applies to everyone in a certain education system. These two factors are closely related and depend on each other for an educational system's success and are addressed throughout this section as case studies in this book.

Section two is about creating a supportive school community and all the issues that arise with this within school districts. It is the hope that all students using this book would be able to develop, articulate, and implement a shared vision of learning that they continuously share with their school communities.

For ease and convenience for classroom use, each case study is divided into seven parts:

Title
School district demographic
PSEL Standards

Background
Issue
Dilemma
Questions

PROFESSIONAL STANDARDS FOR EDUCATIONAL LEADERS (NPBEA, 2015) Summary

Standard 1. Mission, Vision, and Core Values
Effective educational leaders develop, advocate, and enact a shared mission, vision, and core values of high-quality education and academic success and well-being of each student.

Standard 2. Ethics and Professional Norms
Effective educational leaders act ethically and according to professional norms to promote each student's academic success and well-being.

Standard 3. Equity and Cultural Responsiveness
Effective educational leaders strive for equity of educational opportunity and culturally responsive practices to promote each student's academic success and well-being.

Standard 4. Curriculum, Instruction, and Assessment
Effective educational leaders develop and support intellectually rigorous and coherent systems of curriculum, instruction, and assessment to promote each student's academic success and well-being.

Standard 5. Community of Care and Support for Students
Effective educational leaders cultivate an inclusive, caring, and supportive school community that promotes the academic success and well-being of each student.

Standard 6. Professional Capacity of School Personnel
Effective educational leaders develop the professional capacity and practice of school personnel to promote each student's academic success and well-being.

Standard 7. Professional Community for Teachers and Staff
Effective educational leaders foster a professional community of teachers and other professional staff to promote each student's academic success and well-being.

Standard 8. Meaningful Engagement of Families and Community
Effective educational leaders engage families and the community in meaningful, reciprocal, and mutually beneficial ways to promote each student's academic success and well-being.

Standard 9. Operations and Management
Effective educational leaders manage school operations and resources to promote each student's academic success and well-being.

Standard 10. School Improvement
Effective educational leaders act as agents of continuous improvement to promote each student's academic success and well-being.

Section I

EQUITY ISSUES

Case Studies

Chapter 1

The Goose and the Gander

Suburban District
Standards: Community of Care and Support for Students, 5a; Meaningful
   Engagement of Families and Community, 8i

BACKGROUND

The Two Rivers Public Schools are nestled in an idyllic area of the state.
The rivers run clear most of the year, and the community sits on top of a
natural aquifer. Most people seeking to live in Two Rivers want to live in a
wholesome area—one that is natural, clean, and free from crime. The town
of Two Rivers is a top choice for many because of its convenience to access
two major metroplexes in the area. It's a pleasant diversion from the hustle
and bustle of the city.

The residents in Two Rivers love their community. They are conscientious
about their environment and pride themselves on looking out for each other
as neighbors. They are proud of their schools, too.

The district has an enrollment of 6,193 students. The teachers have a
class size that averages 19.2 students, which is 2 students higher than the
state class average. The average experience in years for the teachers is 11,
and their average salary is $48,698. The district has met all accountability
requirements, including surpassing the state graduation rate of 89% with an
impressive 98.1% and averaging a 24.9 on the ACT and 1677 on the SAT.
Less than 5% of the students receive bilingual or ELL instruction, and the
at-risk population is 22.4%. Less than 10% of the students are in special
education.

Table 1.1 Other Demographics Include the Following

African American	9.8%
American Indian	0.4%
Asian	1.7%
Hispanic	20.6%
Pacific Islander	0.2%
White	63.5%
Two or more races	3.6.%
The student population is 63.5% female and 36.5% male.	

ISSUE

The Two Rivers Public School District provided a good educational experience for the children enrolled in its schools. Student achievement was high, the graduation rate was impressive, and the teachers seemed generally satisfied with their work environment.

Even discipline issues were at a minimum—certainly nothing like what the parents had heard happening in the bigger cities in which they worked.

The only problem in Two Rivers Public School District centered around a topic no one had suspected: bullying.

Some of the students targeted their bullying against the LGBTQIA community. This demographic was estimated to be 4.2% of the student enrollment district-wide, but the number was hard to verify. Only a few of the students were willing to speak up about their sexual preferences. Most of the LGBTQIA students hid their gender identification and sexual preferences. They understood all too well that their peers would pick on them relentlessly.

That was already the case with some of the high school and middle school boys. They liked to pick on what they assumed were the weaker students. These boys called the students they suspected of being LGBTQIA by foul names, played nasty jokes on them, and tried embarrassing them in front of their peers.

The boys—and some of the girls—taunted the LGBTQIA students.

One of those students was Matty Smith.

Matty was only a fourth grader, but he was certain he should have never been born a boy. His school records identified him as "Matthew Smith," but everyone, including the teachers, called him Matty.

Matty loved hanging out with the girls, and he even wore dresses to school "to fit in better."

His parents recently won the right for Matty to use the girls' restroom instead of the boys' restroom. Getting the approval had been a big ordeal, and they had fought for Matty to feel like he belonged. The school administration, at the superintendent's urging, conceded to the request.

The girls' parents were concerned about having a boy in the girls' restroom, but the school worked out a schedule so Matty could use a specific restroom at specific times during the day, and the teachers made sure the girls didn't use the restroom during those times.

Things finally quieted down, and education continued.

DILEMMA

One morning Matty Smith was found unconscious in the girls' bathroom.

Two girls had gone to the restroom, and they found Matty lying on the floor, half in a stall and half out. Their shrieks alerted a nearby teacher, Mr. Robinson, who came running to the scene. He looked at the scene and dialed 911. Then he sent the girls to the administration office to get Principal Moses.

As soon as the ambulance took Matty off to the hospital, Principal Moses called the superintendent, Dr. Sheila Anderson, to tell her what had happened.

QUESTIONS

1. Did the superintendent and campus administration make the right decision in letting Matty use the girls' bathroom?
2. What does the data presented in this study tell you about the district? What other data would you want to review if you were the superintendent?
3. The district has a "no-cell phones on campus" policy for employees, but Mr. Robison used his phone to call 911. Is he a hero, or should he be in trouble for violating district policy regarding mobile phones?
4. How likely is it that Matty was unconscious in the restroom because he was a victim of an assault or an incident of bullying?
5. What is the superintendent's next step(s)? How should she communicate with the parents? What about the media?

Chapter 2

Not My Problem

Rural School District (one elementary, one middle, and one high school)
Standards: Community of Care and Support for Students, 5a; Ethics and Professional Norms, 2e; Meaningful Engagement of Families and Community, 8c, i

BACKGROUND

You've been in this small rural district for several years, and you have quickly become a part of the community. The town has a local diner, a fast-food restaurant, a small grocery, a single gas station, a hardware store, and a few other shops. It's the kind of place where everyone can't help but know each other.

The high school has an open campus policy for lunch because most of the students can either walk home for lunch or visit one of the local establishments to grab a bite. Fridays are always busy days for eating out.

The community sticks together and helps each other out whenever they can. The previous year saw torrential rains, and when the middle school flooded, the community came out to help with the cleanup and get the building ready for classes as soon as possible.

Some of the dads brought their BBQ grills and cooked burgers and hotdogs, while others hauled out debris, mopped, and rebuilt some of the walls. Even many of the students helped get their building back in shape.

Review these documents and meeting summaries before planning your next steps:

A letter from the PTA president
Phone messages taken by your administrative assistant
Requests from various school clubs and organizations

In addition, you are meeting with the local Lions Club president when a call comes in from the town marshal.

Letter from the PTA President:

Date: October 11
Subject: This Year's Turkey Shoot

As you know, Thanksgiving is only around the corner, and I probably don't have to tell you that hunting season is about to open soon. I hope your aim has gotten much better than it's been in previous years!

This year, we'd like to have some great prizes to give out to some of the students participating in the shoot, so we're asking for donations from our local businesses and dignitaries. Our students appreciate the recognition they get in the form of trophies, cash prizes, and other goodies, like the orange hunting vest you donated last year.

I'm hoping we can count on your assistance again this year by way of a donation. We'd also be honored to have you serve as one of the judges at the Turkey Shoot, if you're available on November 17.

And by the way, are you OK with us having a gun safety meeting at the high school one evening?

Phone Messages

Message 1

From: Olga Lefstedt, Lead Elementary Cafeteria Worker
Date: October 12
Time: 9:07

Reported smoke coming out of the ovens. Unplugged everything, but can't prep a hot lunch until the ovens are checked. We can make PBJs instead. Please advise.

Message 2

From: Banks Middleton, Lions Club President
Date: October 12
Time: 11:25

Running 15 minutes late. Be there soon.

Message 3

From: Lyle Coffee, High School Principal
Date: October 12
Time: 11:32

Bus 115, on the field trip to the zoo over in the big city reports a flat tire. Do you want to send a repair vehicle or have the driver use the district purchase card to get it fixed?

Message 4

From: Your Assistant
Date: October 12
Time: 11:45

Headed over to the diner to grab lunch, call me if you want your usual, and I'll bring it back for you.

Requests

Request 1: The high school Future Farmers of America (FFA) would like a donation for its annual fund-raiser, Moo Scholarships.

Request 2: The middle school band boosters are selling chocolate bars to raise money for new uniforms. How many bars will you take?

Request 3: The Ladies Home and Garden Club would like you to sponsor a rose bush at the annual garden walk. Can they count on you?

Request 4: Can you speak at the Career and Technology Club next Tuesday at 3:00 p.m.?

Request 5: How many raffle tickets do you want from the elementary science club? They are $1 each, and the club is raffling off an aquarium, complete with fish and supplies.

Meeting Summary with the Lions Club President, Banks Middleton

Banks has been in your office for the past 20 minutes with two important goals in mind. First of all, the Lions Club has once again raised money for eyeglasses for the needy children. Every fall the club donates eyeglasses, and every spring it offers a graduating senior a scholarship. This year, the club is prepared to donate 50 pairs of prescription eyeglasses for children who need them.

In addition, Banks wants you to join Lions. He asks you every time he sees you, and each time he becomes a little more insistent. It's not that you don't want to be part of a civic organization, but it's that you also enjoy having a little time to yourself, which can be hard to come by in a small town.

Just as you are about to tell Banks your response to his invitation, your personal cell phone rings.

You look at the caller ID. You say, "I'm sorry. I have to take this. Go ahead, Mac."

The town marshal Mac Bledsoe is on the other end of the line.

"Where was he when you found the gun? You're sure it wasn't on school property? Okay, then this one is in your hands."

ISSUE

Several issues are to be taken care on this particular morning, from handling broken cafeteria equipment to getting a flat tire fixed on a bus in a nearby city. The bus is carrying students on a field trip.

In addition, several local organizations want your attention, your time, and some of your money.

The Lions Club president is in your office when the city marshal calls you on your personal cell phone about a high school student who has a gun.

DILEMMA

Although you will need to respond to all of the requests that have been made, the most pressing issue is the gun. You need to diffuse the situation, finding out the specifics of what's involved. To make matters more interesting, the Lions Club president is in your office, listening to what you talk over phone. He may be able to hear the marshal's voice as well.

How do you handle the situation?

QUESTIONS

1. Which of the problems the superintendent faced that day were not his or hers to deal with? Why?
2. How would you address each of the challenges for the day? Which are high-priority issues? Which are not? Why?
3. How would you handle the gun issue? Is it a problem if the student is in possession of a weapon but is not on campus? Why or why not?
4. Would you ask the Lions Club president to leave your office so you could speak privately with the marshal?
5. Is it OK to have your assistant pick up your lunch while she's on her lunch break? Why or why not?
6. What is your response to the requests made of you?

Chapter 3

Unsafe Environment

Urban School District (8 elementary schools, 3 middle schools, and 2 high schools)

Standards: Community of Care and Support for Students, 5a, b; Ethics and Professional Norms, 2e; Meaningful Engagement of Families and Community, 8c, j

BACKGROUND

For some time there have been rumblings across the district about the leadership style of one of your school principals, Patricia Ramos. She has been the principal at Williams Middle School for five years, longer than you have been the superintendent in this district.

When you looked at her evaluations over time, you noticed that she was identified as an adequate principal—neither satisfactory nor unsatisfactory. Her campus scores were average across the district, and nothing in particular stood out about her leadership, other than rumors that were beginning to surface.

Some of the talk had been that when she met individually with her teachers, they often left her office in tears. She was described as calculating and cold, and many of her teachers try transferring to other schools within the district each year. This trend has not seemed to bother Ms. Ramos.

The principal is characterized as someone who takes long lunches, arrives late at school (at 8:30 or 9:00 a.m.), and leaves early (sometimes right after lunch).

In addition, there are rumors that Ms. Ramos is having an affair with one of the high school principals, but there has been no confirmation of the relationship yet. That lack of evidence has not kept students and staff from making guesses about it on social media pages.

Review these documents and meeting summaries before planning your next steps:

An e-mail from the fire marshal Bob Rawlings
A request from Patricia Ramos to take off the Thursday and Friday before spring break
A letter signed by several of the teachers at Williams Middle School
A work injury claim form regarding an incident with the Williams Middle School assistant principal
An e-mail from one of the high school principals, Max O'Neil

E-Mail from the Fire Marshal Bob Rawlings

To: Superintendent
From: Bob Rawlings, Fire Marshal
Date: February 22
Subject: Safety concerns at Williams Middle School

Yesterday we responded to a fire alarm at one of your middle schools, Williams Middle School. We pride ourselves on our quick response time, especially when students and the adults who care for them are at risk.

Upon our arrival at the scene, we discovered that a fire had broken out in the art building. It's all cinder block, but everything inside was quite flammable. Fortunately, no students were injured, and many were gathered around the burning building. I understand that Assistant Principal David Rice was quite the hero, trying to put out the fire before we arrived. From what I understand he will recover from his injuries.

That leads me to another concern, however. Are you aware that Principal Ramos makes a practice of chaining and locking all the exterior doors of the building during the students' lunch periods? That may explain why all the students were outside during the incident, but I must remind you that the chaining and locking the doors from the inside is a safety violation.

If I find them chained again, I will have to close the campus until you can guarantee that the doors will remain unlocked for student entry and exit.

I've got to tell you that it's a little disturbing to experience the cold and clinical atmosphere that has developed at Williams. When I was a student there, the school was warm and open—quite a welcoming place to be. How things change over time!

Request from Patricia Ramos

To: Superintendent
From: Patricia Ramos, Principal at Williams Middle School
Date: February 23
Subject: Requesting permission of personal leave

I need to take two personal days right before spring break. I know we're not supposed to take time off right before a holiday, but I have some pressing matters that need my attention. Could you please let me know before this Friday if the days will be approved?

Thanks in advance!

Letter Signed by Several of the Teachers

To: Superintendent
From: Teachers
Date: February 19
Subject: Unsafe conditions at Williams Middle School

Several of the teachers here at Williams Middle School are extremely concerned about safety conditions.

Last week one of the students, an eighth grader, brought a gun to school. It was a pistol. He had it inside the waistband of his jeans, and he brandished it in class. One of the teachers in our group tried to report it to the principal, but she said she was too busy to come to the classroom. Finally, a hall monitor escorted the student to the office, but we have no idea what happened to the student. The student was back in the classroom the next day as though nothing happened.

We have heard several rumors about gang riots possibly happening here at our campus, and we are concerned about violence. We are turning to you for assistance.

Please know that we like working with students and their families. We just want to know that our work place is safe for everyone.

Respectfully,
(Signed) L. Bookman, M. Hernandez, J. Maxwell,
R. Thigpen, A. York, B. Brown
PS: Principal Ramos does not know that we wrote to you, and we would like this report to be anonymous so that it doesn't affect our evaluations.

Work Injury Claim Form

Worker's Compensation Incident Report
Date completed: February 22
Injured employee's name: David Rice
Job title: Assistant principal
Location of accident: Williams Middle School, outside the art building
Time: 12:17
Did accident occur on school property? Yes
Injury reported to: Nelly Perkins, school nurse
Date reported: Feb 22
Body part injured: Burns on right hand and lungs

Describe in detail how injury occurred: The principal handed me a fire extinguisher and directed me outside to the art building. When I flung open the door using my right hand, I realized the doorknob was hot, but I couldn't let go right away, and it burned my hand. I turned away from the flames and heat, thinking I ought to call 911 instead to get a fire truck to help with the fire, but Ms. Ramos told me she didn't want anyone to know there had been a fire. She wanted it handled on the campus. She called me a *pinche mariposa* and said anyone who is a real man would go in and fight the fire. I went back into the smoke and flames, but couldn't breathe and came back out. My lungs feel like they are on fire, and it's hard to breathe.

E-Mail from One of the High School Principals

To: Superintendent
From: Max O'Neil
Date: February 22
Subject: Time-off request

I am making a formal request to use two of my personal days so that I can be absent on the Thursday and Friday before spring break. I've already put them into the system, so if it's not OK, let me know ASAP.

Thank you in advance for your immediate attention to this!

ISSUE

Principal Ramos approaches campus leadership in a laissez-faire manner. She delegates responsibility to others because she herself is often away from the campus. When she is at Williams Middle School, her decision-making processes do not take into account the best interests of the students, faculty, and staff.

When a fire broke out on campus, Principal Ramos tried to prevent the fire department from responding to the call because she wanted to handle the problem at the campus level without bringing in outside support.

DILEMMA

Principal Ramos has placed the safety of students and adults in jeopardy by ignoring safety protocols on the campus. Based on the documents gathered so far, she may even have made several poor choices regarding incidents that could be considered dangerous.

You are faced with a letter from the fire marshal suggesting that he's ready to close down the school, concerns from teachers about safety at campus, and an injury report from one of the assistant principals.

The only group you have not heard from are the parents.

Now Ms. Ramos and another principal are requesting that their personal leave be approved; they have requested the same days.

How do you handle the situation?

QUESTIONS

1. Why is chaining the school doors and locking them a problem? Can the fire marshal actually close the school building?
2. How do you propose investigating the situation regarding Ms. Ramos? Whom do you need to speak with? Why?
3. Should you address the purported relationship with the high school principal? Why or why not?
4. What options do you have in dealing with Ms. Ramos's behavior? What is the best course of action? Why?
5. Would your responses be different if Ms. Ramos claimed that she was being discriminated against because she is a Hispanic female? Why or why not?
6. How should you follow up with the fire marshal? What about the parents?

Chapter 4

Busing Issues and Budget Cuts

Suburban School District (12 elementary schools, 5 middle schools, and 2 high schools)

Standards: Equity and Cultural Responsiveness, 3b, c, e; Community of Care and Support for Students, 5a; Operations and Management, 9c, i

BACKGROUND

As the new superintendent of schools in a trendy suburban school district, you have been charged with making some major budget cuts in an effort to set aside money for other upcoming projects. Your evaluation and your contract likely depend in part on the success of these cuts.

You've asked for a summary of program costs and their possible reductions, and now you have the data in front of you. You intend to cut transportation expenses because no routes within a two-mile radius of the school are reimbursed by the state. This has always been an expense borne by the district.

Review these documents and meeting summaries before making your recommendations:

A chart showing possible budget cuts

A summary of the bus routes

Table 4.1 Chart of Possible Budget Cuts

Program	Current Expenses	Proposed Cuts
Salaries	$43.2 million	0
Professional development	$5.3 million	$100,000
Supplies and materials	$8.9 million	$400,000
Transportation	$23.2 million	$12 million

Summary of parent meeting
Superintendent scorecard results

Summary of Bus Routes

Your school district expands across 32 square miles, and approximately 210 bus routes run every morning and every afternoon to transport students to and from school.

It has long been the district policy to provide bus service for all students, regardless of how close they live near the school. The elementary school principals have reported that when they are on bus duty in the mornings, they see school buses stop in front of the school to pick up waiting children, so they don't have to cross the parking lot. This seems like excess to the elementary school principals, and it does to you, too.

In addition to the regular routes, there are 21 special education buses that also transport students, and any children involved in extracurricular activities also require bus services.

Summary of Parent Meeting

At a town hall parent meeting in August, you proposed to follow the state recommendation of providing transportation services only to those students who lived two miles or more away from their school of attendance.

The parents groaned unanimously; many began arguing about unsafe routes, and they described the busy roads the students would have to travel on.

Other parents complained that their children were too young to walk to school that far. They could not walk with them and did not have transportation of their own. In addition, some of the parents with special needs students were concerned about getting their children to school now that not all students will be picked up by the buses.

The parents did not want cuts made in transportation. They took to social media, complaining that you are more interested in saving money than saving their children's lives. The media picked up the story, and they have been following and reporting your decisions.

Superintendent Scorecard Results

The district has made it a tradition to grade the superintendent with a public scorecard. Every superintendent has undergone this transparent process, and the results are also used for the superintendent's annual evaluation and contract renewal.

Your latest scorecard results are as follows:

Table 4.2 Professional Standards for Educational Leaders

STANDARD	*Score*
STANDARD 1. MISSION, VISION, AND CORE VALUES Effective educational leaders develop, advocate, and enact a shared mission, vision, and core values of high-quality education and academic success and well-being of *each* student.	8.2
STANDARD 2. ETHICS AND PROFESSIONAL NORMS Effective educational leaders act ethically and according to professional norms to promote *each* student's academic success and well-being.	9.8
STANDARD 3. EQUITY AND CULTURAL RESPONSIVENESS Effective educational leaders strive for equity of educational opportunity and culturally responsive practices to promote *each* student's academic success and well-being.	8.9
STANDARD 4. CURRICULUM, INSTRUCTION, AND ASSESSMENT Effective educational leaders develop and support intellectually rigorous and coherent systems of curriculum, instruction, and assessment to promote *each* student's academic success and well-being.	9.4
STANDARD 5. COMMUNITY OF CARE AND SUPPORT FOR STUDENTS Effective educational leaders cultivate an inclusive, caring, and supportive school community that promotes the academic success and well-being of *each* student.	6.9
STANDARD 6. PROFESSIONAL CAPACITY OF SCHOOL PERSONNEL Effective educational leaders develop the professional capacity and practice of school personnel to promote *each* student's academic success and well-being.	8.8
STANDARD 7. PROFESSIONAL COMMUNITY FOR TEACHERS AND STAFF Effective educational leaders foster a professional community of teachers and other professional staff to promote *each* student's academic success and well-being.	8.9
STANDARD 8. MEANINGFUL ENGAGEMENT OF FAMILIES AND COMMUNITY Effective educational leaders engage families and the community in meaningful, reciprocal, and mutually beneficial ways to promote *each* student's academic success and well-being.	7.0
STANDARD 9. OPERATIONS AND MANAGEMENT Effective educational leaders manage school operations and resources to promote *each* student's academic success and well-being.	6.5
STANDARD 10. SCHOOL IMPROVEMENT Effective educational leaders act as agents of continuous improvement to promote *each* student's academic success and well-being.	9.0

ISSUE

Transportation cuts are easily the quickest way to set aside district money for other projects. The district's policy of providing transportation to every student, regardless of the distance he or she lives from the school, is an expensive one.

The parents, with the support of the media, have mounted a campaign fighting your decision on cutting transportation for students.

DILEMMA

You have held your ground in cutting transportation costs in the district, but now the superintendent scorecard has been released for public review. In some areas, you scored exceptionally well, but in others, the community has expressed its concern with your decisions. The school board has been divided in the transportation cuts issue.

You will be meeting with the school board next week in advance of your annual evaluation. What do you need to tell them?

QUESTIONS

1. What information are you missing in regard to the budget cuts? What else do you need to see? Why?
2. How can you explain your vision for transportation to the parents? What legitimate concerns do they have?
3. How can you find common ground with the parents and community?
4. What do you tell the school board? Do you think your evaluation is in jeopardy? Why or why not?

Chapter 5

Town Hall Meeting

Rural School District (6 elementary schools, 3 middle schools, and 1 high
  school)
Standards: Equity and Cultural Responsiveness, 3c, f; Meaningful Engagement of Families and Community, 8c, g; School Improvement, 10a

BACKGROUND

You are the new principal at a rural school district. The parents in the community respect the schools for the education it provides, and many of the
parents themselves are humble because most do not have college experience.
Regardless of their own educational limitation, they want the best for their
children, and they are passionate advocates for the children in the community.

You have decided to hold three town hall meetings—one for parents of
elementary-aged children, one for middle school children, and one for high
school children.

At the middle school town hall, you discover some interesting information.

Review these documents and meeting summaries before making your
recommendations:

A summary of the events at the middle school town hall meeting
The textbook inventory report for middle school 2, the school in question
State assessment scores for middle school 2

Summary of the Middle School Town Hall Meeting

You have already held one town hall meeting, for the elementary school
campuses, and it went well. The parents seemed happy to meet you, hear

about your vision for their children's academic success, and visit with you afterward.

Your middle school town hall meeting was quite different, however. After introducing each of the principals of the three middle schools, you noticed immediately that principals 1 and 3 received thunderous applause when you announced their names. Each spoke for a few minutes, and again there was applause. When you introduced principal 2, however, the applause was sparse, and there was no applause after she spoke—only an awkward pause.

During the town hall meeting, you spoke of many of the same things you covered at the elementary school meeting, but when you asked for questions or concerns, one of the parents spoke up. "Should our children have textbooks? And other instructional materials?"

"Of course," you replied. "And which school are you from?

"Middle school 2."

Several other parents stood up to be recognized. They said they too were from middle school 2. Their children were not allowed to have books. They could not check out textbooks. Library books were off limits, too. They could be read only at school.

"I'd like to address that," said the principal. She walked to a microphone and explained to the audience that in order to protect the instructional materials, students could use them only during the day, unless parents wanted to reserve a book for $50. When the book was returned, so was the $50.

"You know this has been our policy for several years," she said.

Textbook Inventory Report

You ask the textbook coordinator to provide you with an inventory list for middle school 2. Any missing books are to be paid for by the campus. This is the report you were handed:

Table 5.1 Inventory and Assessment Scores

Year	Number of Missing Math Books	Number of Missing Reading Books	Number of Missing Science Books	Number of Missing Social Studies Books	Number of Missing Library Books
A	54	89	17	15	836
B	103	117	43	38	3,759
C	24	31	24	16	43
D	12	14	3	0	5
E	0	1	0	0	0

Table 5.2 State Assessment Scores for Middle School 2

	Math	Reading	Science	Social Studies
Middle school 1—Year C	89	92	86	94
Year D	90	94	88	92
Year E	94	95	90	93
Middle school 2—Year C	74	82	78	88
Year D	67	84	75	86
Year E	65	79	71	77
Middle school 3—Year C	96	97	95	99
Year D	97	99	93	97
Year E	96	99	96	98

ISSUE

You decided to hold town hall meetings to greet the parents and community in the school district, and let them get to know you and understand your mission and vision for the schools and their children.

At a town hall meeting, you discover that one of the middle school principals has been hoarding instructional materials. She refuses to permit students to take home textbooks or library books unless the parents pay a refundable deposit.

The principal insists that her policy has significantly reduced the number of lost books. The parents want their children to have access to the instructional materials.

DILEMMA

The parents want their children to have access to textbooks and other instructional resources. The principal of middle school 2 has withheld instructional resources form the students, permitting them access only during school hours. They are not allowed to take school resources home with them.

The middle school principal insists that she has done an outstanding job as the steward to district resources at her campus because for the past several years, she has lost no textbooks or other resources. She feels as though she deserves kudos for her decisions in this area. You had no idea that this had been her practice.

QUESTIONS

1. Are the parents right in requesting that students have access to instructional resources at home? Why or why not?

2. Has the middle school principal done an outstanding job of protecting district materials? Why or why not?
3. How might the principal's decision have affected the assessment scores on the campus? What's the correlation? What evidence supports your analysis?
4. What other implications are there for not permitting students extended access of instructional resources?
5. What are the next steps you will take regarding the principal of middle school 2?
6. How can you keep parents advised of your decisions, and what they can expect from the campuses where their children attend school?

Chapter 6

Goodbye Is Forever

Rural School District (3 elementary schools, 2 middle schools, 1 high school)
Standards: Community of Care and Support for Students, 5a, b; Equity and
   Cultural Responsiveness, 3a

BACKGROUND

Felicia Walker was the superintendent of the Riverton Rural School District,
and she was just beginning her second year in the position.

The first year, Mrs. Walker spent time at the six campuses in the district,
getting to know the principals and their concerns. She felt like she had built
rapport with each of them. This year, Mrs. Walker wanted to extend that
feeling of rapport with the community itself. She especially wanted to get to
know some of the culturally diverse groups in the district, including a few
refugee and immigrant families who moved to Riverton in the past year.

When the phone rang, Mrs. Walker was not expecting what she heard.

"Repeat what you told me, but talk slower." She told the caller. "Did you
call 911?" she asked. "What about the parents? Keep the students in their
classrooms for now. I'll be right there."

As Mrs. Walker arrived, a police car and an ambulance had just pulled up
to the elementary school building. She hurried into the building and followed
them.

A five-year-old student was unconscious in the gym. The paramedics tried
to resuscitate the child and placed him on a stretcher and then took him back
to the ambulance, where they continued their life-saving efforts. The boy,
Johnny Timson, had been pronounced dead on arrival at the hospital. He had
hanged himself from a bleacher with his belt. Perhaps it was on purpose, or

perhaps he had been playing a game with his belt and he snagged it on the bleacher.

Mrs. Walker, the principal, and the police officer paid the parents a home visit and offered assistance to the family. On the way to the boy's home, the superintendent decided to cancel classes for the rest of the day at the school.

The police conducted an investigation at the school and found no evidence of foul play. The death was ruled as accidental.

Mrs. Walker went back out to the parents' home to check on them and see how they were doing. On the second visit, she learned a few more details about the family:

> The man the mother was living with was not Johnny's father. He was the current boyfriend. The father had committed suicide four years ago.
>
> Johnny had an older brother named Rick, but Rick, too, committed suicide two years ago. He had been in middle school when it happened. The parents thought the suicide was Rick's way of escaping the bullying he suffered.

The family had no money saved for funeral expenses and a burial.

Mrs. Walker returned to her office, and she asked her assistant to set up a Go Fund Me account for Johnny Timson. Next, she called the head counselor in the district and asked her to coordinate grief awareness session for any campuses, students, or staff needing them, especially at Johnny's former campus. Then she called the funeral home to see if she could arrange a discount for the child's casket and burial. The district would send flowers.

The superintendent then sent out this e-mail:

To: All employees
From: Mrs. Walker, superintendent
Date: March 10
Subject: Arrangements for Johnny T.

It is with a heavy heart that I tell you that our second elementary school experienced a death of one of its students. Johnny T. lost his life yesterday and will be greatly missed by all those who knew him.

His death was a suicide. You may be surprised to learn that very young children can and will take their own lives, but it is something we must learn more about and prevent because every one of our children is precious. In the weeks and months to come, we will engage in a series of professional development trainings that will help us better understand how to prevent suicide.

In the meantime, we have grief counseling available for anyone who needs it.

Johnny's funeral will take place this Friday at 10:00 at Cedarwald Cemetery. I realize that you cannot all attend the ceremony, but know that a district representative will be present. In the meantime, if you would like to donate to the family, please click on this Go Fund Me link.

The news of Johnny's death in the small rural district went viral, and like most small rural communities, the residents banded together to help support the family.

It wasn't long, however, that some of the district employees noticed that Mrs. Timson was driving a Mercedes. The car was a couple of years old, but it was still an expensive vehicle. Her boy brought home a new truck, and yet the district was donating heavily to the family's burden of expenses.

Teachers began posting snarky comments in their social media pages about how the family was purportedly using the money. Their comments could easily be considered bullying.

Mrs. Walker had also asked the counselors to prepare a report regarding bullying and suicidal ideations at each of the campuses. This is what she received from the counselors:

Table 6.1 School Safety Inventory

Campuses	No. of Incidents of Bullying	No. of Suicidal Ideations	No. of Self-Harming Incidents
Elementary school	356	19	27
Middle school	1,517	87	214
High school	996	73	109

It seemed like her next steps were clear and evident.

ISSUE

An elementary school student has committed suicide at school. The family has a history of suicides, and they seem to be as a result of bullying. In an effort to become more involved in the community, Mrs. Walker has visited the family several times, offered funeral and burial assistance for the child, and she has set up a Go Fund Me account for the family.

The teachers have noticed that the family of the deceased have bought new vehicles and are spending money in ways that had not been done before. The teachers made bullying comments about the family in social media.

DILEMMA

The teachers are bullying the Timsons through passive-aggressive posts in social media venues, but Mrs. Walker has also noticed a correlation between bullying and self-harm, which the counselor's research indicates is a valid concern. To protect the children in the district and give teachers the tools they need to confront the problem, Mrs. Walker will have to take action.

QUESTIONS

1. Was Mrs. Walker out of place in setting up a Go Fund Me account? Why or why not?
2. Should Mrs. Walker have sent out the e-mail about the deceased student? Why or why not?
3. What should Mrs. Walker do about the teachers who are bullying the Timsons online about the new spending habits? What should Mrs. Walker do about the Timsons unusual purchases? Why?
4. What should be Mrs. Walker's next steps? What training should Mrs. Walker provide the campuses? Why?
5. How can Mrs. Walker involve the community in the issue of bullying and self-abuse?

Chapter 7

Discipline Diligence

Urban High School
Standards: Equity and Cultural Responsiveness, 3a, c, e; Community of
Care and Support for Students, 5b; Professional Community for Teach-
ers and Staff, 8c

BACKGROUND

Safety and discipline management at Danforth High School seemed to be in
a downward spiral.

Teachers complained to the school administration that they spent so much
of their time redirecting students that there was precious little time left to
teach. Even when they did have time, there was only a small group of students
interested in learning anything, anyway.

Quite a few of the teachers taught to that small group at the front of the
classroom, letting the rest of the students do pretty much anything they
wanted at the back of the room as long as they didn't kill anyone or have
sex.

When behaviors got out of hand, the teachers would write a referral and
send the troublemaker and sometimes his squad to the office.

The office would take one look at the students—it was always the
same 15% who were sent from class—and the assistant principal would
either let the students wait out the class in the office or suspend them for
a few days, giving everyone a much-needed break. No one—the teachers
or the administrators—thought much about their approach to "resolving"
the problem until the day Roberta Brown showed up and wanted to see
the principal.

Mrs. Brown marched into Principal Jackson's office, armed with several big planning calendars and a black Sharpie. She dumped the calendars on Mr. Jackson's desk but kept the Sharpie in her right hand.

Then she walked behind the desk and stood next to the principal, who remained in his chair, and was too stunned to move.

"Let me show you something, sir," said Mrs. Brown. "It's about my boy Antwan. You may remember that he was suspended yesterday."

Principal Jackson racked his brain, trying to remember if either of the assistant principals mentioned Antwan. It did seem like Antwan was always in trouble for something, so his suspension would not have been a surprise.

Mrs. Brown dug a beat-up calendar out of the pile.

"You see this?" she asked. "This is the year Antwan was in fifth grade. He was suspended for seven days that year." She uncapped the Sharpie and drew an exceptionally large "7" on the cover of the calendar.

"Now look at this," she said. She pulled out each calendar, indicating the number of days Antwan had been suspended each year. Each time she called out a year and the number of days Antwan had been suspended, she wrote the number on the front of the calendar.

6th grade, 16 days
7th grade, 22 days
8th grade, 31 days
9th grade, 47 days
10th grade, 38 days
11th grade, 52 days

Mrs. Brown walked around to the front of Mr. Jackson's desk. "Now, you are a smart man—how many days is that?" she wanted to know.

Mr. Jackson looked at the numbers. There had to be more than 200 days of school that Antwan had missed. He flipped through the top few calendars. Each absence had been marked with a big black X, drawn with the Sharpie, no doubt.

"If you came up 211, you'd be right," said Antwan's mother. "That's more than one entire school year. Just how is my child supposed to learn anything if you keep suspending him from school? He has already missed MORE than an entire school year thanks to your people. And now he is supposed to be close to graduation? He doesn't even want to be here anymore."

Mr. Jackson didn't say anything.

Mrs. Brown continued. "Antwan is reading at a 7th grade reading level. His math scores, according to your own tests, are at the 5th grade level. It seems to me that the only thing you are preparing him for is failure in life. He can't read, he can figure it out, but he does understand that because he's black, he gets in trouble more than the other kids whose skin is lighter and whiter."

"Now Mrs. Brown, you can't accuse us of suspending your son because he's black," said Mr. Jackson.

"Oh, I can and I am," said Mrs. Brown. "And I have a petition signed by more than 100 families who feel the same way. We all want to see the discipline data you have regarding suspensions, because we think it's time to do something about it."

Some of the discipline reports the school had gathered included the following *percentages* of referrals for the current school year:

Table 7.1 Infraction Types by Race

	White	African American	Hispanic	Asian	Pacific Islander or Native American
Tardies	48	23	32	2	0
Skipping class	15	52	31	0	0
Bullying	11	63	26	0	0
Unprepared for class	9	50	41	0	0
Insubordination	5	65	30	0	0
Theft	7	55	39	0	0
Cheating	14	54	32	0	0
Possession of illegal substance	5	60	35	0	0
Possession of weapon	0	80	20	0	0
Vandalism	15	62	23	0	0
Dress code violation	30	40	37	1	2
Public display of affection	35	35	37	0	3

Table 7.2 Infraction Location

	White	African American	Hispanic	Asian	Pacific Islander or Native American
Classroom	5	75	20	0	0
Hallway	10	60	20	5	5
Office	15	50	35	0	0
Cafeteria	5	70	25	0	0
Restroom	10	65	25	0	0
Lockers	15	45	40	0	0
Music room	45	15	40	0	0
Art room	25	25	50	0	0
Gym	10	65	25	0	0
Computer lab	10	40	50	0	0
Parking lot	35	30	35	0	0
Bus loading/unloading	5	70	25	0	0

Table 7.3 Actions Taken

	White	African American	Hispanic	Asian	Pacific Islander or Native American
Verbal warning	50	20	40	100	95
Written warning	20	10	20	0	5
Time-out	10	5	10	0	0
In-school suspension	5	10	5	0	0
Out-of-school suspension	3	30	15	0	0
Sent to alternative education placement (in district)	1	15	5	0	0
Sent to alternative education placement (out of district—juvenile detention or residential treatment)	1	10	5	0	0

ISSUE

Discipline management at Danforth High School is inequitable. The teachers have given up in trying to redirect behaviors, and students do whatever they want in the classroom and in the halls. When students are sent to the office with referrals, they either wait out the class time by sitting in the office or they are suspended.

Both practices have proven ineffective, but they have not gone unnoticed. Some of the parents have been particularly observant of their own children's behavior consequences and also of the administrations' practices in general.

The racial disparity in how students are treated is obvious.

DILEMMA

Mrs. Brown, the mother of Antwan Brown, has been keeping a record of her child's suspensions from school for several years. It's a practice that she began when Antwan was in the fifth grade, and now she has a record that her son has been suspended more days than there are in a single school year.

She wants the principal to review the data for discipline at his campus. She also has a petition with the signatures of more than 100 parents who also want a closer look at the practices of assigning consequences for misbehavior. They feel as though African American students are especially targeted for the most extreme consequences.

Mrs. Brown has also accused the school district of being at least partly responsible for Antwan's inability to read or calculate on grade level, noting that he no longer wants to be in school.

QUESTIONS

1. Should Mr. Jackson get the parents involved? Why or why not?
2. What other data should the school administration consider reviewing? Why?
3. What data can the school share with parents? What data can they not share?
4. How should Mr. Jackson report back to the concerned parents? How can he involve them?
5. How accurate is Mrs. Brown's assessment that the school system is at fault for her child not being on grade level?

Chapter 8

Empire Builder

Suburban School District (1 elementary school, 1 middle school, 1 high school)

Standards: Equity and Cultural Responsiveness, 3a, b, c; Meaningful Engagement of Families and Community, 8g

BACKGROUND

Delilah Johnson was an educator with the mind of the businessperson. She was perfectly suited for the position of superintendent because she not only had a passion for instruction, but she also understood the business aspect perhaps better than anyone else.

When she became the superintendent at Golden Heights School District, she recognized immediately that the district would have trouble making ends meet. It was a tiny suburban district boasting a single elementary, middle, and high school. Mrs. Johnson felt fortunate she didn't also have to serve as a high school principal. Had that been the case she wouldn't have time to develop new business interests.

It was going to be business interests that would save the district money and improve her salary. She couldn't imagine a better win–win solution.

As to be expected, most of the district funds came from the local tax base, and some from state and federal money. As a result, most of the funds were spent on employees' salaries, particularly those of teachers and auxiliary personnel.

Mrs. Johnson intentionally kept the superintendent salaries very low. She knew that it looks good to the community and that the school board appreciated the fact that she was not a gold digger.

She wasn't. She had plenty of other ways to make money.

One of them that she had been looking into for some time was to apply for a district-sponsored charter school. This school would be located out of district so that it was not in home competition with Golden Heights School District. It would not be trying to attract the same students.

Mrs. Johnson knew how to write charter petitions that would get approved. The first petition she wrote was for an elementary school in the neighboring county. When she explained her proposal to the school board, she told them that because of high mobility opportunities in the area, parents often moved from county to county. Golden Heights School District was such a small district that parents often did not consider it as a viable option for their children because there were so many larger and more well-known school districts in the area. A charter school in the neighboring county would give the school district name recognition and respect.

By opening a second school, Golden Heights School District could attract more children to its district.

The school board was excited about opening a new school. A charter school could rent an existing building and get off the ground in no time. That's exactly what happened with the first Empire Charter campus.

The state then printed the petition, and Golden Heights School District had added a fourth campus.

What many people did not realize, however, is that the state also permitted authorization for districts like Golden Heights to charge an administrative fee not exceeding 3% for the oversight and administration of the new campus.

Superintendent Johnson made sure that the school board saw the 3% in fees that the new school generated. Empire Charter School 1 brought Golden Heights an additional $30,000 that first year.

"Just imagine what it would be like if we could open even more schools," she said.

The school board was excited to think about the possibilities.

Within the next three years, Golden Heights, under the leadership of Superintendent Johnson, opened seven more schools, all of them charters, and all of them out of district.

For her efforts, she requested from the board a small stipend for each school that had been opened. They agreed.

Table 8.1 Superintendent Salary and Stipend Request

Year	Golden Heights Salary	Empire Stipend
1	$95,000	$5,000
2	$102,000	$20,000
3	$109,000	$40,000

Mrs. Johnson didn't stop there. To staff each of the Empire Charter schools, she hired a close friend or family member. It didn't matter that these employees did not have a professional education certification, because charter schools did not require professional certification. Besides, each of them had access to Delilah Johnson. Of course, anytime she was consulted on matters she also charged a small fee. For each hour Mrs. Johnson spent consulting with Empire Charter schools, she charged an additional $125/hour. The school board was unaware of these additional charges because they were billed as consulting hours to the district and paid for professional services she offered.

While attending a conference for school superintendents, Mrs. Johnson sat in on a session about increasing school revenue. The speaker alerted the audience to a shell game played by some school districts and their superintendents. The deception included opening a large number of charter schools in order to obtain the administrative fee allowed by law, thus padding the school district's coffers as well as the superintendent's.

The school board president turned to Mrs. Johnson and asked point-blank, "Is that what you're doing?"

ISSUE

The Golden Heights School District consisted of three schools. It was a tiny district by most standards, but their new superintendent, Delilah Johnson, saw an opportunity to bring more money and name recognition to Golden Heights. With the board's approval, she began writing charter school petitions to open charters schools in nearby counties. Because Golden Heights would have to oversee the charter schools, the district could charge an administrative fee.

Mrs. Johnson put most of the fees earned back into the Golden Heights education program, but she kept part of the fees for herself.

DILEMMA

The school board president was attending a superintendents' conference with Delilah Johnson. In one of the sessions, he learned that some school districts and their superintendents play a shell game in which they move money around from campus to campus. This movement is made particularly easy when there is an outside charter involved.

The school board president recognized that Mrs. Johnson had been charging the district a stipend for working with the campuses. This money came from the money that the Empire Charter campuses generated. He does not yet know that Mrs. Johnson also has been charging Empire Charter other fees as well, but Mrs. Johnson knows that he soon will.

QUESTIONS

1. Is it considered nepotism if Mrs. Johnson's relatives work outside Golden Heights but for the Empire Charter schools? Why or why not?
2. Could Mrs. Johnson's actions be considered a conflict of interest? How so?
3. Which of Mrs. Johnson's actions are illegal and why? Which are not good business practices and why?
4. Why would the school board president be at a conference for superintendents?
5. What could Mrs. Johnson do to avoid the appearance of money laundering and fraud?

Chapter 9

Beyond Bullying

Urban School District (46 elementary schools, 16 middle schools, 7 high
schools)

Standards: Equity and Cultural Responsiveness, 3a; Community of Care
and Support for Students, 5a, b; Mission, Vision and Core Values, 1g

BACKGROUND

George Garza, the superintendent of City Center School District, liked it
when the campus principals upheld the mission vision and core values of
City Center. The district prided itself on the simple statements that seemed to
epitomize everything they did: all students safe, all students lifelong learners.

It was exactly those two things that were important to Dr. Garza. First and
foremost, he expected every campus, elementary, middle, or high school, to
place its student achievement at the forefront. That meant if students needed
help in reading or mathematics, they got it. If students needed help in any
academic area, there was a caring and compassionate adult ready to step in
and help out.

As a result, most of the students in the City Center schools performed well
on their state assessments and other national exams.

The other thing that Dr. Garza expected for every student in one of his
schools was that they would be safe. Student safety was a big concern in
the community as well. The Simpson's Urban School District students often
walked to school, and some of them used public transportation. Schools
routinely offered seminars on safety to parents and children. In addition, the
teachers and other school professionals were taught how to recognize unsafe
events and collaborate as a team to problem solve around them.

The biggest initiative put on by the school this year was an anti-bullying campaign.

Every school reported monthly on how well they were doing with this new initiative. The counselors routinely taught anti-bullying lessons, the teachers supported these efforts and provided maintenance activities in the classroom, and school administrators worked diligently to lower the amount of bullying taking place on the campus and at extracurricular activities.

Dr. Garza encouraged the campus leaders to tweet and make other social media posts about how effective the anti-bullying campaign was at each of their campuses. The principals as a whole reiterated the district motto in their posts: all students safe, all students lifelong learners.

In the spring semester, Dr. Garza requested a student survey to be completed at each campus. He had heard from the school administrators how well the anti-bullying campaign was going, but now he wanted to receive feedback from the students themselves. The superintendent was suspicious that the posts he was seeing in social media were not an accurate representation of what was actually going on at the campuses.

Students who were bullied would not be likely to make public comments about their experiences. He hoped that they would reveal more information in an anonymous survey.

The campuses headed to week window to distribute the surveys and get the results back to the central office for disaggregation. Unfortunately, the entire process was delayed because of an event at single elementary campus Public School 107.

A nine-year-old boy by the name of Malachi Jones committed suicide in the boys' restroom on the second floor of the school. It was possible that at the last minute he changed his mind; he had staggered out of the restroom, reached out toward a couple of passers-by, and fell to the ground. More than a dozen people walked by, without noticing Malachi on the ground to assist him.

The school principal Tim Jensen found the student and called 911. As soon as this student was en route to the hospital, Mr. Jensen called Mrs. Jones, Malachi's mother, and asked her to meet him at the hospital.

The news media also met the principal and the mother at the hospital emergency room, where Malachi was pronounced dead.

In remembering Malachi, the school counselors and teachers reflected back on the work they had done with the student. Malachi often visited the counselor's office with complaints about the other boys in his class. He reported that they called him names and taunted him, making fun of the way he dressed and wore his hair.

At the funeral, Malachi's English teacher gave the boy's journal to Mrs. Jones. The mother was surprised when she read the content lamenting about how isolated her son felt at school.

"And you never thought to report this?" she asked her son's teacher.

"I never read the journal," said Malachi's teacher. "Those are the private thoughts of the children, and we don't grade those journals. There is no reason to read them either."

The superintendent was standing next to the teacher when she made her statement. He wanted to talk to both the teacher and the campus principal.

When Dr. Garza returned to the office later that day, there were two reports on his desk. The first one contained the results of the bullying survey. The campus reports regarding monthly discipline incidents were also ready for his review.

Table 9.1 Survey Results

Questions	Elementary	Middle School	High School
Percentage of students never bullied at school	10	8	12
Percentage of students bullied in the past week	82	94	78
Percentage of students bullied in the past month	85	96	84
Percentage of students bullied in the past three months	80	89	77
Percentage of students bullied in the past six months	87	92	83
Percentage of students bullied online	54	67	91
Percentage of students bullied in class	75	88	86
Percentage of students bullied in the halls	78	89	90
Percentage of students bullied in the restrooms	89	95	75
Percentage of students bullied in the gym	56	87	75
Percentage of students bullied in the cafeteria	58	77	63

Table 9.2 Campus Reports—No. of Incidents of Bullying in the Elementary Schools*

School Number	August	September	October	November	December	January	February	March	April	May	June
101	1	3	2	3	1	4	2	1			
102	2	2	0	0	0	2	1	0			
103	1	2	2	3	2	4	2	1			
104	4	3	7	3	2	1	0	1			
105	2	1	5	3	1	0	2	0	TBD		
106	3	0	2	1	0	3	0	1			
107	0	0	0	0	0	0	0	0			
108	2	2	1	3	0	1	0	0			
109	1	0	2	3	0	1	0	2			

*Not all elementary schools have been listed.

ISSUE

The anti-bullying campaign at City Center School District was the largest single initiative undertaken by the district this year. Dr. Garza, the superintendent, brought all of the campus principals together and inculcated the belief that the mission and vision of the district was completely achievable: all students could become lifelong learners, and all students could be safe.

This was not the case at one of the elementary schools, where a student who had been repeatedly bullied committed suicide at the campus.

DILEMMA

The school principal Tim Jensen failed to contact the superintendent when a student safety issue of great magnitude occurred at the campus. As a result, the news media asked the superintendent for a statement about the child's death before the superintendent knew what happened.

In addition, the school district had spent the year promoting the success of the anti-bullying initiative, and yet the student's death was attributed to excessive bullying.

When the superintendent of schools reviewed the data regarding the student survey and the campus reports, two unique facts stood out to him. First, the students reported a higher rate of bullying than the campus administrators had reported. Second, the campus of the deceased student reported that there were no bullying incidents that year.

QUESTIONS

1. Which age group of students is experiencing the most bullying? Why do you think that is the case?
2. Which areas of the school are the most dangerous for bullying? Why? What should be done about it?
3. What, if anything, should the superintendent say to the media? Why?
4. Imagine that you are the superintendent of the City Center School District. Give your statement to the media about the incident that has taken place.
5. What conversation does the superintendent need to have with the principal Tim Jensen? What would you say? Why?
6. What's the problem with the bullying data submitted by the campus principal? Why is this a problem?

Chapter 10

A Whale of a Challenge

Suburban School District (7 elementary schools, 3 middle schools, 1 high school)

Standards: Community of Care and Support for Students, 5a, b; Meaningful Engagement of Families and Community, 8c, g, i

BACKGROUND

The executive director for student services Ron Booth requested a meeting with Superintendent Annie Littleton. When the superintendent asked what the meeting was about, the executive director wouldn't say directly, but did let his boss know that he needed to see her about a very serious matter.

At the meeting, Mr. Booth laid the following information on the desk in front of the superintendent.

"What is this?" she asked.

"This is a table telling the amount of time counselors have been spending working with students over the last three months," said Mr. Booth. "You'll notice a significant increase in not only the contact hours, but also of worrisome events, including suicidal ideations."

"We want our counselors counseling, do we not?" asked the superintendent.

"Yes, of course, but wait until you hear what the issue is," said Mr. Booth.

The superintendent looked at the report. It was a compilation of data from all the counselors across the district. The data from 11 different campuses—elementary, middle, and high schools—was comingled. Not only was there an increase in the contact hours and reportable events (outcries suggesting imminent danger), but the events were also becoming far more serious with each passing month.

Table 10.1 Report of Counselors' Contact Log Hours and Reportable Events

Month	Contact Hours	Threats of Physical or Psychological Self-Harm	Threats of Physical or Psychological Harm to Others	Suicidal Ideations
September	880	5	0	3
October	1,195	13	8	17
November	1,725	142	26	49

"Alright, Mr. Booth. What's causing this?" asked the superintendent.

"It's the Blue Whale Challenge," said Mr. Booth.

Mrs. Littleton took off her reading glasses and looked at the director. "A few years ago it was cinnamon. Kids were choking on it," she said. "Now it's whales?"

"No, it's more than that. It's about progressive physical and psychological harm," said the director. "And it always ends in suicide."

The director went on to explain that the Blue Whale Challenge had begun in another country. Players interested in this game connected with the facilitator in an online forum. Over the next 50 days, they were given a series of directives aimed to gauge their devotion to the game and willingness to undergo severe physical and psychological ordeals. Each ordeal had to be documented digitally and sent to the facilitator who would then assign the next task.

At first, the tasks were simple and innocuous. For example, the participant might be asked to walk along a busy street or prick his or her finger with a needle. Later he or she would be asked to skip school and watch horror films all day, carve the outline of a whale on his or her hand, and worse. As each day passed, the participants were required to engage in riskier behavior, until the 50th day, when the participant was challenged to commit suicide.

"How many students are playing this game?" asked the superintendent.

"As of now, only eight students have admitted to playing the game. It's odd, though. We believe that more students are involved. Usually, students confess to wrongdoing because they are either scared or the confession is a badge of honor. No one is willing to open up about this," said Mr. Booth.

"How many do you suspect are playing the Blue Whale Challenge?" Mrs. Littleton asked.

"As many as a couple of hundred," said the director.

"Find them," said Mrs. Littleton.

That same day, the superintendent drafted the following letter to be sent to the parents of every student in the district. It read:

November 30

Dear Parents and Guardians, Teachers and Administrators:

As you are aware, nothing is more important than the safety of our children.

I want you to be aware of a new challenge or "game" that some students may be participating in. It's called the Blue Whale Challenge, named after the sea creatures that beach themselves and die. We do not know who is responsible for this game, but believe that it may have its origins in another country, where over 100 children have reportedly committed suicide.

The facilitators are operating this game in an attempt to annihilate the population and eradicate the world of those who are easily controlled.

The counselors at our school have seen an increase in self-harming behaviors and threats of harm against others. Some of our students have already threatened to commit suicide. The counselors have contacted you if your child is one of those players wanting to take his or her life.

We are closely monitoring the children at school to make sure they are not engaging in risky behaviors here. I encourage you to do the same at home.

Please call my office or the counselor at your child's school if you think your child has accepted the challenge. We want to help.

Annie Littleton

ISSUE

The student services director has informed the superintendent of schools that the counselors across the district have been very concerned by the recent student behaviors they have seen. Not only have the counselors experienced an increase in the number of counseling hours requested by students, but they have also noticed an increase in self-harming behaviors, threats to harm others, and suicidal ideations.

This increase has occurred in the past three months.

DILEMMA

The superintendent has recognized that the Blue Whale Challenge is a real threat to the safety of children in the school district.

The student services director provided the superintendent of schools with counseling data showing a significant increase in services for students. This increase has been in conjunction with the discovery of the Blue Whale Challenge.

The superintendent wanted to send a letter to parents the same day she discovered what was going on. She also wanted to inform other agencies of the imminent danger the challenge could present to students.

QUESTIONS

1. What outlets can and should the superintendent use to get the word out about the Blue Whale Challenge?
2. How much detail should the parents be told about this game? Why? What would you ask the superintendent to leave out of her letter to the parents? Why?
3. What advice or support would you give the campuses as they learn more about the challenge and intervene on the behalf of their students?
4. What steps should be taken if the adults suspect students are engaged in harmful behaviors? What other agencies should be involved and why?
5. What other steps can the district take to stop the Blue Whale Challenge?

Chapter 11

Special Attention

Suburban School District
Standards: Equity and Cultural Responsiveness, 3a, c, e; Community of
    Care and Support for Students, 5a, b

BACKGROUND

The High Cliff Unified School District wanted to say that its High Cliff
hawks were respected learners and leaders of the future.

District leadership thought that it went without saying that all students in
the district were to be respected because they could all learn and lead.

Superintendent Brad Lawson often said that he learned as much from students in the community as he hoped they were learning from him. The other
administrators in the district, as well as the faculty, felt pretty much the same
way. At least, most of them did.

There were still a few teachers and even a principal or two who still needed
to be convinced of the statement. It turned out that Ma'shuq, a sixth-grade
student at one of the middle schools, would be the one to teach everyone.

Ma'shuq had been identified as a special education student since second
grade. He had been referred for services in kindergarten and then again in
first grade, but the district wanted to make sure that it was not a language
interference causing the delay in Ma'shuq's learning. He was diagnosed with
a severe speech impediment that made it impossible for him to pronounce
certain sounds in English—or French or Arabic, which were the other two
languages he spoke. He also had developmental delays and a learning disability in reading.

School was hard for him.

Ma'shuq was getting support through special education services. The speech therapist met with him three times a week, and Ma'shuq received help in reading from a special education teacher. He also met with a counselor once a week to help him learn how to make friends.

Making friends was hard for Ma'shuq. Many of the students in his class teased him because of his speech impediment. They called him names, ignored his requests for help, refused to sit with him at lunch, and taunted him during recess.

Ma'shuq began to slip into depression. He didn't want to go to school, he was no longer eager about learning, and he had no friends. His English teacher, Mrs. Newly, saw what was happening, and she voiced her concerns to another teacher who also taught Ma'shuq.

"Aw, you know, boys will be boys. He'll figure it out eventually," said math teacher Mr. Fenster.

Just days later, Ma'shuq sat in Mrs. Newly's classroom, sobbing. He refused to go to his math class next period. Mrs. Newly took her student to the counselor's office, and she returned to her classroom to fire off an e-mail aimed at Mr. Fenster.

In the e-mail Mrs. Newly reminded the math teacher that Ma'shuq had an individualized education plan that had to be followed. She expressed her concern that by ignoring Ma'shuq's requests for help, the math teacher was also ignoring some of the requirements in the Individualized Education Plan (IEP) for helping Ma'shuq cope with his peers.

When Mrs. Newly saw that Ma'shuq's IEP was still not being addressed, and that the bullying had gotten worse, she notified the principal of the problem. Again, she put her concern in writing.

"By the way, you are aware that he brings a lot of bullying on himself, right?" wrote the principal in a response to the teacher's concern. There was no other follow-up until Ma'shuq had an emotional outburst in the math classroom. He toppled over a computer, causing it to shatter, and he knocked over several desks and chairs as he ran out the door.

The principal suspended him from school without holding a manifestation determination.

When Ma'shuq refused to return to school, his parents became even more distraught. They contacted the counselor, who told them that she had done everything she could. Perhaps they could consider medication to calm their son down?

When Superintendent Lawson found out about the situation, he was furious. He hated being blindsided like this, with no indication that trouble had been brewing. This was certainly not how respectful learners and the leaders were created. He was even more furious when he was notified that Ma'shuq's parents were suing the school district for being out of compliance with their son's IEP.

Those named in the lawsuit included Mrs. Newly, Mr. Fenster, the counselor, Principal Bowman, the special education director, the boy's bus driver, and the superintendent himself. Ma'shuq's parents also filed a civil suit against the parents of the boys who bullied their son. They were seeking $75,000 in damages.

The superintendent contacted the district legal counsel immediately. After reviewing the situation, the attorney for the school district told Superintendent Lawson that the parents had a particularly good case. In fact there has even been a precedent for lawsuits just like this. In the attorney's opinion, it was time for the superintendent to notify the school board that they would likely lose this case, and that it would generate a lot of negative public attention.

Superintendent Lawson didn't know who to be the maddest at first.

ISSUE

The campus principal at the High Cliff Unified School District Middle School has largely ignored the volatile situation on her campus. One of her special education students has been bullied because of his disability. The principal and at least one other teacher have written off behavior, suggesting that bullying is just how some boys behave. The principal also noted in writing that the special education student does things to make students want to bully him.

Only one teacher steps forward, concerned about the child's IEP that was not being followed.

The parents were also concerned that the IEP was not being followed, especially when he had been suspended from school without a manifestation determination meeting after having an outburst in the classroom where he damaged school property.

DILEMMA

The parents are now suing the school district for its failure to comply with their child's IEP. The lawsuit names a variety of district employees, and the parents are also filing a civil suit against the parents of the children who bullied their son.

The superintendent was unaware of what had been going on at the campus, and he did not know that anyone was out of compliance with the IEP.

He now will have to work with the irate parents, let the board know what is going on, and find a solution to the problem.

QUESTIONS

1. Who is at fault in failing to meet Ma'shuq's social, emotional, and academic needs? Why?
2. Why was expressing concerns in writing about the student and the IEP appropriate in this situation?
3. Was it appropriate for the counselor to recommend that the child take medication? Why or why not?
4. What type of professional development training would you recommend for the campus principal? The counselor? What about all of the other principals and counselors in the district?
5. Was the superintendent liable for the IEP being followed? Why or why not?

Chapter 12

Hasta La Vista, Everybody

Suburban School District; Standards: Mission, Vision, and Core Values
1f; Equity and Cultural Responsiveness 3h; Professional Capacity of
School Personnel 6 i

BACKGROUND

Carol Hughes had just completed her sixth year as the superintendent at the
Knickson School District. She had been hired after one year experience as an
assistant superintendent. And she moved across the state to take this position
at Knickson.

During her interview, she asked about the former superintendent who was
leaving. The school members looked sheepishly at each other, and some of
them looked at the floor. Finally, one member spoke up to explain that the
outgoing superintendent had been fairly headstrong and had run into some
conflicts with the school board members, as well as with those who work in
central office administration. There were irreconcilable differences between
the superintendent and those trying to support his work.

Hughes felt as though she was fairly easy to get along with, and she
knew how to communicate well with others and overcome differences in
order to get the job done. She did not think it would be a problem working
with any of her cabinet from central office, with members of the school
board, and with other employees across the district, as well as people in the
community.

During her first year, Superintendent Hughes worked hard to develop relationships with all of the stakeholders in the district. She held the retreat for
her cabinet so that they could work on creating a shared vision for the future

55

of the district. The team spent a couple of days together creating the focus that would drive the district forward.

Next, Superintendent Hughes regularly met with members of the school board for lunch. She was careful not to meet with too many board members at one time so that the lunches could not be considered a meeting at which there was a quorum present. For that reason, she could not take members of the school board on a retreat.

During her first year, Hughes was able to get everyone to focus on the unified vision created by the leadership team, and engage in instructionally based and instructionally supportive activities that would propel the district into being a powerful educational resource.

Her work was effective. At the end of the second year, the school board offered Superintendent Hughes a five-year contract to lead the district.

It wasn't too long after that until the curriculum director Katie Stevens began complaining about the workload she was forced to endure. The superintendent expected that Stevens would regularly visit every campus to meet with the campus administration teams, that she would be a part of curriculum writing events, and that she would be on call during the state assessment testing windows.

Stevens said, "It's really too much to ask." "In the past I was never expected to do all of these things, and now it's like the district owns me. Why don't the other directors have to work this hard? What about the HR director? He always takes long lunches and gets to go home on time. It's not even like he does any real work, you know."

"It's your job," said the superintendent. "If you no longer want it, please let me know, so I can begin looking for your replacement."

The transportation director, too, complained about his extra workload. Superintendent Hughes asked him to provide regular reports on fuel usage and maintenance of the district's vehicles; updated training lists; and the identification of any trouble areas, such as student behavior on the buses.

When the transportation director commented that that seemed like a lot of additional work, the superintendent reminded him that by applying for this job he had asked for all of the duties that come with it. She also pointed out that his contract said "and other duties as assigned."

"You're just picking on me because I don't work in the same building with the rest of you," said the transportation director.

The straw that broke the camel's back, however, was the election of board member John West two years ago. Ever since John West came on the school board, the members were more antagonistic toward each other. He created infighting among the board members.

The school board could not complete discussions while in session because West always asked obscure questions and then tried to filibuster the answer to his own questions so that the issue became muddled and no decision could be reached.

In frustration, his colleagues would table issues until the next meeting, pushing agenda items further and further away from being decided upon. Ultimately, the delayed decisions were hurting the ability of the district to move forward with initiatives and strategies.

This year West was up for reelection, and it looked like he was favored to win.

"That would be the worst possible thing for the school district. I cannot imagine a less qualified or incompetent individual to serve on the school board," said Superintendent Hughes.

When West found out that Superintendent Hughes had commented on his competence for his position on the school board, he hired an attorney because he felt her statements defamed his character and limited his likelihood of being reelected. He intended to sue the superintendent for slander.

The superintendent of schools decided that she had had enough of the backstabbing and infighting within the school district. She needed a long vacation, one where she could sort out her thoughts and think about her next steps.

ISSUE

The previous superintendent of Knickson School District resigned because of infighting within the central office administration and with members of the school board. The inability to get along between departments within central office and the school board had been pervasive.

Superintendent Hughes felt that she could change all of that. She spent her first year in the position building relationships across central office and with every member of the school board. She had been highly effective, too. Everything had seemed to settle down, at least for a few years.

The infighting resumed, and people began complaining about their jobs. A newly elected school board member also stirred up the drama among the school board members. And all of a sudden the school board could not make decisions or get anything done.

DILEMMA

Superintendent Hughes was getting tired of seeing how everyone treated each other, both in her cabinet and on the school board. She had done a lot of work to build trust and understanding among employees and community members. Now they acted as though they had never gotten along with each other.

The worst offender was the newly elected school board member, and it looked like he would win this election and retain his seat on the board.

The superintendent thought it would help if everyone went on vacation and let off some of the stress that had been building up.

When the employees returned from summer vacation, the superintendent's administrative assistant unlocked her boss's office door to put the mail on her desk. She was shocked at what she saw.

Every personal item and every trace of Superintendent Hughes was gone. The only thing that remained there were the items belonging to the district, including the superintendent's laptop and the keys to the district's vehicles.

A letter was found on the desk. It was from the superintendent.

She had resigned, effective immediately.

QUESTIONS

1. Why did the infighting start again? How could the superintendent have prevented it?
2. How should the superintendent have handled the curriculum director?
3. What about the transportation director? Were the requests out of line? Why or why not?
4. How could the superintendent keep the board members on track? What should be done about West?
5. Why could not the superintendent take the school board members on a retreat to work on team-building activities like those she did with central office members?
6. How should the superintendent have handled her resignation? Why?

Chapter 13

Not to Blame

Suburban School District
Standards: Ethics and Professional Norms, 2d; Equity and Cultural Responsiveness, 3h; Meaningful Engagement of Families and Community, 8c

BACKGROUND

Wally Tarsi was the superintendent of schools in the Kingsland Community School District. He had been in this position of leadership for the past seven years, and he did not plan on going anywhere else, not anytime soon.

His valuations each year had been fine, with just a couple of things to work on, but that was expected especially when leading a large suburban school district. There were always challenges to be overcome and battles to be fought. Tarsi knew this because he lived through most of them. He was pretty sure he would live to fight another day.

That's how he saw most of the problems he faced—as an ongoing fight. That's what he did in order to make this school district known for its outstanding academics and athletics. He was a constant advocate for the community and the schools. He supported the teachers, the school administrators, and he was a huge advocate of how hard they worked with the students in the district.

Many people in nearby communities recognized the superintendent's drive and determination in creating an excellent school district. They wanted to transfer their children into the Kingsland Community School District because they knew their children would get a great education and have wonderful experiences.

The superintendent had faced some rocky times. He had been accused of sexual discrimination, opting to hire a man for a position instead of the woman who was far more qualified for the job.

He mishandled a special education case that drew advocacy groups to the district on behalf of a special needs child. The boy required an one-on-one teaching assistant, and as the child entered the middle school, Superintendent Tarsi refused to allot an full-time employee (FTE) to the child, arguing that the teaching assistant had been assigned to the elementary school, and that's where she would stay.

Tarsi explained that it was not his fault that he didn't understand how much the child needed the assistant. When he met the boy for the first time, Tarsi remarked, "Other than the fact you are sitting in a wheel chair, you seem just fine to me."

When several positions for bus driving opened up, the superintendent recommended to the transportation director that he would like his college-aged son to be given one of the jobs.

He said, "Bradley's a good kid, in college you know, and trying to make ends meet. You know how it is."

The transportation director hired the superintendent's son and helped him become licensed to drive a commercial vehicle. Bradley had done pretty well on his driving test, and to celebrate that night, he got stoned.

The next morning when he reported to work, his eyes were bloodshot, and he acted high.

"Dude, I got this," he said as he climbed into the driver's seat. The director had Bradley physically removed from the bus.

"I had no idea. Seriously. I don't see how that could be my fault," said the superintendent.

In another incident, when one of the high schools had a fund-raiser activity for one of its students who had been injured in a serious car accident, Tarsi insisted on helping out at the grill, and he donated pork hotdogs. The student was a Muslim, and much of the Muslim community had turned out for the event. Even the non-Muslims were disgusted with the superintendent's level of callousness and disregard for the cultural norms in his community.

Tarsi responded to the outcries by pointing out that no one had told him the fund-raiser was for a Muslim student.

When a position for the director of federal programs opened up, Tarsi recommended that his wife be considered for the position.

"I honestly know of no better candidate," he said. He made arrangements for her to ace the interview and be installed as the new director, but he was not present when the board approved her contract.

"I stepped away for only a moment," said Tarsi, "and the school board took action without me being present. I had no idea they were going to do such a thing. Can you imagine?"

After only a few months had gone by, Mrs. Tarsi had already let several funding opportunities slip by, and she had "forgotten" to file some of the reports required by federal law. The district lost $900,000 and appeared on the state's monitoring radar.

The superintendent stopped by his wife's office, furious about what had happened. He slammed the door shut behind him, and there was a loud crash. Pictures fell off the wall in his wife's office, and something crashed and shattered in the office next door as well.

"How *could* you!" the superintendent shouted.

His wife froze.

"Do you realize that you just lost the district nearly $1 million? Where do you think that money is supposed to come from? Do you think we have that kind of money just lying around? There are salaries to pay, and expenses to take care of. You screwed this up for both of us," snarled Superintendent Tarsi.

"Well it's not like I had any training," said his wife. "I got thrown in here, and was told to do the best I could. This was the best I could do."

"Are you kidding? The best you can do is get me run out of the district? This isn't even fair it's not my fault. It's your fault," said Superintendent Tarsi. And with that the superintendent pulled back his arm and clenched his fist.

At that moment, the finance director walked in and looked at the superintendent.

Superintendent Tarsi lowered his arm.

"I'm calling the police. And then I'm calling the school board president," said the finance director.

ISSUE

Superintendent Tarsi has been in the school district for seven years. He has earned a reputation as being someone who can get the job done. He has created an excellent academic and athletic program in the district, and the community is very pleased with what he has done.

Unfortunately he just had some difficulty along the way. Not all of his decisions have been good; some of the decisions have cost the district considerable amount of money. He has been involved in lawsuits and other difficulties. There have been situations in which he has shown little tact and no compassion. He has also hired two family members to work in the school district.

DILEMMA

Superintendent Tarsi has made a series of bad decisions. Each time he has made one of these bad decisions, he explains it away by saying that it is not his fault. The superintendent does not take blame for any other problems or challenges that he creates.

One of the most recent problems occurred when he hired his wife as the federal programs director. In a few months' time she missed several deadlines for reporting and receiving federal funds. The district was poised to lose nearly $1 million, which was necessary for operations.

Furious, the superintendent stormed into his wife's office and cocked his arm, ready to punch her.

The finance director walked in, saw what was happening, and called the police.

QUESTIONS

1. Identify the smallest mistake Superintendent Tarsi made. Why is this mistake not a problem?
2. What is the biggest mistake that Superintendent Tarsi made? Why?
3. In what ways did Superintendent Tarsi alienate the community?
4. Do you agree that Superintendent Tarsi is not to blame for some of these mistakes? Why or why not?
5. What do you think Superintendent Tarsi can expect to happen next?

Chapter 14

More Than Money

Rural District
Standard: Meaningful Engagement of Families and Community, 8h, i

BACKGROUND

Like many other superintendents in her state, Dr. Lisa Bentley is feeling the pains of not having enough funding for school programs and initiatives. The Meadow School District has always offered a diversified curriculum. Students took classes in a variety of fields, and they had ample opportunities to gain new experiences.

Meadow School District had a rigorous curriculum consisting of opportunities to earn dual credit, learn a foreign language, play sports, and engage in the arts. Students also had a wide range of extracurricular clubs from which to choose.

All of that was coming to an end.

Once again, the state education agency announced imminent cutbacks in funding. The rural districts would likely be hit the hardest, since they received less in taxes and federal funding.

Meadow School District receives approximately $1.5 million in Title I funding and less than $15,000 in bilingual/ESL funding.

Other funding cuts included:

• Local	• +2%
• State cuts	• −3%
• Federal	• N/A

o Title I	o −7%
o Technology	o −14%
o Special education	o +4%

Dr. Bentley has served on a steering committee consisting of superinten-dents and businesspeople across the state. They have been meeting for the last year to discuss the issues facing schools, including living expenses, inflation, and reductions in formula funding. As frustrating as it was to see financial support shrivel up, the committee felt energized because they were exploring new options with open minds.

Some of the options included increasing sales tax, initiating a variety of property tax algorithms, and floating bonds to carry the districts further down the road.

Several committee members, including Dr. Bentley, have been of the opinion that increasing state funding by a mere $1 per pupil will increase the property values of the residents in their communities by at least $20.

"For every dollar we get," said Dr. Bentley, "we make $19. The investment in education has always been well spent. It always will be. Students get an education, and our communities are rewarded as well."

With all the work that had been done, the steering committee had still not been able to take a resolution to their state legislators.

ISSUE

Even though Dr. Bentley is an ardent advocate of exploring alternative education funding, she and her peers have not been able to come up with a solution that would satisfy most stakeholders when it comes to financing education.

Once again, another school year is starting, and Dr. Bentley must decide where the money will do the most good for the students in the Meadow School District.

In looking over the projections, she decides to eliminate some of the instructional positions first. Her proposal includes eliminating the position of reading specialist at the elementary school. She also wants to eliminate the four librarian positions in the district. To staff the library, Dr. Bentley wants to hire an instructional assistant to serve in this capacity, and the assistant will rotate to a different campus each day of the week.

In addition, Dr. Bentley has decided that eliminating all of the art classes except for those required for high school credit will free up more money in the way of salaries, supplies, and space.

The last change Dr. Bentley will propose to the school board is to eliminate most after-school activities that require paying additional stipends to teachers. Doing away with these activities will also eliminate the need for additional transportation services.

She had a few other suggestions to bring up at the board meeting.

DILEMMA

Dr. Bentley prepared her proposals for the June board meeting. She had talked individually to several board members, revealing that she had come up with a money-saving plan for the district. Each member was in favor of saving money, although they didn't know just yet how it would happen.

When Dr. Bentley's administrative assistant typed up the agenda, the proposal's part about eliminating the librarian positions caught her eye. Her husband was the middle school librarian.

By the time the school board settled into their seats for their meeting, the board room was packed with concerned parents and employees. Some of them had already signed up for discussion time at the beginning of the meeting.

They were already talking among themselves about the apparent lack of transparency and certain inefficiency.

QUESTIONS

1. How serious are the budget cuts? What kind of impact might they have on the district?
2. How should Dr. Bentley have handled her suggestions for saving money? Who should have been involved and why?
3. What are some ways the district could generate funding or reduce spending? Toss out as many ideas as possible, if even they sound crazy at first.
4. Would cutting programs save money? How should Dr. Bentley go about cutting some of the school district's programs?

Chapter 15

Bonding with the Community

Suburban District
Standards: Meaningful Engagement of Families and Community, 8g, h

BACKGROUND

Jack Jacobs had been the superintendent of the La Salle Public Schools for eight years, right at the height of exponential growth in what was once a sleepy little town.

La Salle had always been a small community, one that resisted change, and liked things the way they once were. For that reason, many people fleeing urban areas in search of a better life came to La Salle. It was peaceful—a real slice of Americana.

The school superintendent Jack Jacobs adored the town the moment he saw it. There was a quaint town square, and tourists flocked to it on the weekends. The people who lived in La Salle looked out after each other, and they took pride in their community and their schools.

"I could retire a happy man here," thought Jacobs. He jumped at the chance to lead the district when the school board offered him the top position.

"We want someone who will be here for the long haul," said the board president. "Someone who truly wants to be part of our community."

"That's me," said Jacobs.

Superintendent Jacobs had a vision for the district. He knew that one day the district would no longer be a small town. It would grow into a prestigious community nestled in the suburbs.

In his role as the superintendent of La Salle schools, Jack Jacobs managed to get two bonds passed so far. The first was for a new elementary school, and it was $9.5 million. The second bond had a price tag of $27.2 million, and it would pay for repairs to existing buildings and modernize the athletic facilities.

Now Superintendent Jacobs wanted to get a third bond passed. The price tag for this one is $48.8 million. Some of the larger projects include:

- Building a new elementary school. Cost: $33 million.
- Renovating the oldest campus in the district and turning it into an alternative campus. Cost: $1 million.
- Installing digital marquees at the high school, middle school, and central administration buildings. Cost: $150,000.
- Renovating existing schools. Cost: $12 million
- Purchasing new vehicles for district use, including trucks with lift gates and transportation for the superintendent. Cost: $100,000
- Installing cameras in classrooms for security at each of the campuses. Cost $250,000.
- Renovating the athletic facilities. Cost: $1.25 million.
- Allocating cost for project management. Cost: $1.5 million.
- Purchasing handheld technology devices for students. Cost: $950,000.

Jacobs directed the district IT department to set up a dedicated page on the district website. It was exclusively for distributing information and updates about the bonds.

Superintendent Jacobs also sent a letter to parents in the community that read, in part:

> Our current elementary classrooms no longer meet minimum standards for minimum square footage. They are less than 650 square feet in size, and the new standard for a classroom of 25 students is 750 square feet. We must build a new elementary that can accommodate the greater enrollment.
>
> La Salle School District currently accepts transfer students, but these facilities are not being built for them. We need the new school and the upgrades regardless of whether we accept transfer students or not.
>
> Our new proposed school site will require major site work, including the redesigning of traffic flow on the main roads around the school. A Land Feasibility Study determined that this tract is the best site for a school even if the costs are greater than at any other proposed site.
>
> Should you have any Questions or concerns, please contact at one of the numbers below.

ISSUE

Not everyone is a fan of another bond package in La Salle. Taxes had been climbing steadily because of the influx of new residents.

La Salle has a divided population: half of the households are families with children, and half are retired people on relatively fixed incomes. The families wanted the bond to pass. It would mean improved facilities and programs for their children. They didn't mind paying a little extra in their taxes for that. If things got really bad, they could always move again.

The retirees did not want their taxes to go up, and they worried that if a large population moved out of La Salle and into one of the neighboring districts to pay less in taxes, who would be left holding the checkbook?

After researching the bonds, residents discovered that neither bond was insured, and there was no discussion of the third being insured, either.

The discontent was low key at first, but as the election neared, residents became more vocal about the bond.

DILEMMA

The community has become highly divided over the proposed bond. Many of the residents want everything they need to improve the school facilities for the children here. Some are opposed to any kind of bond. Then there are the handful of residents who understand while a bond may be inevitable, they disagree with some of the items being considered.

There was also talk that this was Superintendent Jacobs's last year in education. He reached retirement age two years ago, and he could leave the district at any time, retiring comfortably. There was fear that he would leave the district altogether, but only after strapping La Salle with $100 million in debt.

"There's no way you'll get another bond passed here in La Salle," said the mayor. "I personally will see to it that your pet projects do not get funded."

Jack Jacobs knew that a new bond was the only way the district would be able to keep up with the tiny town's growth. It was also a way to poise the district for future growth. They might even name a school after him one day.

He had to get the bond passed if the district was going to keep up with the other districts in the area.

QUESTIONS

1. Is it a good idea to post updates on the school website about the current and proposed bonds? Why or why not?
2. What is the benefit of securing funding through bonds?
3. What items in the third bond package could be questionable?
4. Should school bonds be insured? Why or why not?
5. How should the superintendent go about generating interest and support for the next bond?

Section II

SUPPORTIVE SCHOOL COMMUNITY

Case Studies

Chapter 16

Preparing for Diversity

Rural District
Standard: Equity and Cultural Responsiveness, 3 a, b, c

BACKGROUND

Arthur Dumas is the superintendent at Greenmoor Public School District. He has held this position for 12 years. The district encompasses several hundred miles of rural land, and the schools are the main focus in this community. The campuses disseminate information to parents and neighborhoods, and they provide additional student services, such as low-cost vaccinations and year-round library services for students.

"We'd do so much more," lamented Dr. Dumas. "But there's more need than money. Our student demographics are changing, too. I don't know how we'll get everyone the education they deserve."

Dr. Dumas meant his remarks as positive—an attempt to show that he truly cared for the changing population in the community and wanted to meet the needs of the families and their children.

His passion in education focused on two things: advocating for the state and federal funding his students in the district earned and making sure their resources were used wisely. The problem, as he saw it, was that change had arrived, and not everyone had been ready for it. Just a decade ago, the district was 80% white, 10% black, and 10% Hispanic.

Dr. Dumas tried to tell the community that nothing stayed the same forever, not even Greenmoor Public School District and the population it served. As the years had gone by, the population became more diversified, and so did the needs of the students. The data that the superintendent and the principals were looking at revealed some interesting truths.

73

Table 16.1 Percentage of Students by Race and Ethnicity

Data Elements 2017–2018	District/ State	Value	0 --50%--- -------------------------------100%
Percentage of American Indian and Alaskan Native students	District State	0.02 % 0 %	
Percentage of black students	District State	21.2 % 10.1 %	
Percentage of Hispanic students	District State	48.0 % 30.1 %	
Percentage of Native Hawaiian or other Pacific Islander students	District State	0.01 % 0.01 %	
Percentage of white students	District State	29.5 % 59.7 %	

Table 16.2 Total Program Funding

Data Elements 2017–2018	District/State	Amount
Title I/School Readiness	District	$325,000
	State	$8,725,000
State Assessment and Accountability	District	$60,000
	State	$360,000
College and Career Awareness	District	$410,000
	State	$490,000
ELL Education and Bilingual Education	District	$50,000
	State	$700,000
Migrant Services and Education	District	$49,000
	State	$400,500
Homeless and At-Risk Youth	District	$12,000
	State	$202,000
Special Education	District	$3,900,000
	State	$111,750,000
School Turn-Around	District	$200,250
	State	$900,000
Teacher Training	District	$4,000,000
	State	$55,000,000

The attitude of some of the school leaders, however, didn't change.

"Look here," said the high school principal Frank Le Torneau. "We've done a pretty good job educating kids in these parts. That says we know what we're doing. Anyone new to the district will have to adapt to our program."

Several other principals murmured their agreement.

The high school principal continued, "I'd venture to say we do an out-standing job at our schools, and we save the taxpayers plenty of money. Our leftover money at the end of the year gets sent back to Central so they can start the next school year or send it back to the state."

Dr. Dumas squinted his eyes and lowered his reading glasses to look at the principals. Did he just hear what he thought he heard?

ISSUE

Superintendent Dr. Arthur Dumas had seen his rural district change and grow in the 12 years he had overseen the education of the children in his rural community. During this time, he had seen the student demographics change from predominantly white to more diversified ethnicities. Recently the white population was no longer the largest subgroup. There were more Hispanics than any other group in the Greenmoor community.

During his tenure as superintendent, Dr. Dumas had advocated for being prepared for the change that they would one day face.

That change had arrived, but some of his school leaders, especially the high school principal, were adamant that the new students and their families conform to the old way of doing district business. Greenmoor Public Schools had always done a fine job in the past of meeting student needs. The leaders saw no reason to change.

They were proud of the job they were doing.

DILEMMA

Superintendent Dr. Dumas faced a threefold challenge. His student demographics had been changing with each passing year, and so had the funding sources the district received. Culturally diverse students deserved an education that could meet their specific needs, and every dollar was critical for providing that kind of education.

Today was the first time that Dr. Dumas heard the principals brag about continuing their old practices. Many of the leaders seemed unwilling to make accommodations for diversity, and they even sent back unused money for those children.

The schools were not meeting the needs of the changing population. They weren't even keeping up.

QUESTIONS

1. What other data would you like to see presented?
2. Why might Dr. Dumas not have noticed these challenges before?
3. What's the best way to make sure that the students at Greenmoor Public School District receive the services to which they are entitled?
4. What training do the school leaders need? What about the teachers?
5. If you were Dr. Dumas, what are your next steps?

Chapter 17

Publicity, Politics, and Priorities

Suburban School District (1 elementary school, 1 middle school, and 1
high school)

Standards: Ethics and Professional Norms, 2e; Meaningful Engagement
of Families and Community, 8c, d; Operations and Management, 9f;
School Improvement, 10 h

BACKGROUND

As the superintendent of a small suburban school district, you have been
charged with increasing the capacity for integrating technology in classroom
instruction and keeping costs in line.

One of the education trends you'd like to establish in the district is BYOD,
or bring your own device. Having students and teachers bring their own
technology devices can create a seamless approach to using technology 24/7.

The current district practice is to check out a laptop to the teachers, but
each laptop is collected during the winter break and the summer to sweep
them for viruses. The big cleanup takes place in the summer, but that's when
teachers want access to technology so they can prepare for the upcoming
school year and use their devices for professional development opportunities.

Students often don't complete their class assignments involving technology, because the work isn't available at home for them to do. There are not
enough devices available for checking out to each student. The district is not
at a 1:1 student ratio yet.

Many of the students have smartphones and tablets of their own. The teachers regularly write referrals to the office for students who are distracted by

their own devices, and the principals have suspended students for being distracted.

You have discussed a BYOD policy with the school board, and they support your decision to advance the district with this technological approach.

At the next leadership meeting with the campus principals, you propose your idea and ask them to read and discuss the following articles:

- https://thejournal.com/articles/2015/02/10/9-it-best-practices-for-byod-districts.aspx
- https://elearningindustry.com/using-byod-schools-advantages-disadvantages

In addition to the BYOD policy, you would like to see the following happen:

- Weekly podcasts or social media videos by each principal with updates from the campus. Currently the elementary principal writes a weekly newsletter. The middle school and high school principals update calendars on their websites.
- Campus principals and district leaders post an education-related article weekly in LinkedIn.
- Each campus is to create and maintain a Facebook page so that the community and students can interact with the school in social media venues that are timely and appropriate.

The campus principals are willing to consider a BYOD policy for the district, but they are largely unwilling to engage in social media themselves. Their concerns are as follows:

- Social media takes too much time.
- They don't know how to make podcasts or posts.
- They don't want to be attacked by the public.
- Social media should not become a distraction for the students.
- What they are doing works fine; there have been no complaints.
- Their LinkedIn accounts are personal.
- They don't know what to post or to talk about.
- Will this be a part of their evaluation at the end of the year?
- Do they have to use their own devices, or will the district continue to provide them?
- Does that mean they have to respond to social media comments at night and on weekends? They already have to go to school functions. . . .

The PTA president has also written you the following letter:

To: Superintendent
From: Darla Dodson, PTA president
Date: September 19
Subject: Technology devices for kids

   I've been told recently that you are thinking about forcing kids to use their own technology in school. I, like many other parents, am a little concerned by this, especially because not all students have access to technology like some of the richer kids.

   If everyone has to use their own device, what does that mean for students who don't have devices? I have an 11-year-old who has her own phone, but the 5-year-old isn't responsible enough to have a smartphone. So what happens in a case like that? He gets left out, or you are forcing me and other parents to buy more smartphones?

   I don't think that's fair, especially when the district has plenty of money.

   Several of the parents have been asking me about your new plan, and I think it would be great if you could fill us in on some of the details.

   Would you be willing to speak at our next PTA meeting? It's on September 23, at 7:00 p.m.

   There will be plenty of coffee and cookies!

   How would you go about allaying the concerns of each of these groups?

ISSUE

One of your initiatives as the new superintendent is to establish a BYOD policy for the students and employees in the district.

   From everything you have read the BYOD direction could prove to be highly cost-effective, especially over the next three years. Not all of the stakeholders in the district share your enthusiasm, but they are willing to hear you out.

DILEMMA

A BYOD policy is striking terrors in the hearts of parents and administrators alike. In the past, the district has had limited technology devices for use, and a BYOD device would expand the use of technology significantly.

The principals are hesitant to engage in social media, and they are equally apprehensive about letting students and staff bring their own devices to the campuses.

Parents are concerned that they will have to purchase more technology even for their youngest children, thereby creating undue financial burdens on families.

You have not even put the policy in place yet.

QUESTIONS

1. What do the parents need to know about the BYOD policy? Why?
2. How can you get the campus principals onboard with your plan? What training might they need to be successful in meeting your technology goals?
3. If you were to establish a district technology committee, who would be on it and why?
4. What types of things should the technology committee consider? Why?
5. How will you ensure that all students, even the five-year-olds, have access to appropriate technology devices?

Chapter 18

He Said, She Said

Rural School District (3 elementary schools, 1 middle school, 1 high school)
Standards: Professional Community for Teachers and Staff, 7g; Meaningful Engagement of Families and Community, 8a, d, f, h

BACKGROUND

Leonard Matthews was one of two final candidates interviewing for the position of superintendent in Milford County.

Matthews had been a director of student services in another district, and he
felt ready for a positive change. He wanted to be a superintendent of schools,
in a position where he knew he could make a difference for students and for
their teachers.

He had looked around in his own district, but it seemed like there were no
available openings coming up in the near future. Instead of waiting another
three to five years for an opening he may or may not get, Matthews decided
to look elsewhere for openings. He discussed his intentions with the current
superintendent.

Matthews submitted five applications and was interviewed by two school
districts. The first district was a suburban district with several schools at each
level. The board was polite during the interview, but it was obvious that there
was no chemistry between the candidate and his potential board.

When Matthews interviewed at Milford County schools, however, he took
an instant like to the small community and the people in it. He had reviewed
district data and was impressed with what they had done as a district, but
Matthews also saw that they could do so much more. He wanted to lead them
in the right direction.

He felt that there were several groups of students who were disenfranchised from education, and that some of the district practices were exclusive to the students who needed school the most. Matthews could help right the perceived wrongs he saw.

Fortunately, the school board seemed to enjoy talking with candidate Matthews. His answers must have satisfied the members of the school board because they voted to hire him as the next Milford County superintendent. What Matthews did not realize is that the vote was 4–3.

At the first board meeting Leonard Matthews attended, he was surprised to see such a small turnout. The meeting consisted of himself, the school board, a couple of parents, and his new secretary. "Where was everyone else?" he found himself asking.

"Oh, no one comes to the meetings," said the board president. "It's not really necessary you know. If we need information during the week, we just call that member of your cabinet and ask whatever question we need to know the answer for."

Matthews couldn't believe that his cabinet members would not be present at the meeting.

"It usually works out fine," said the president. "Unless Betty here gets her information twisted or forgets to write down what was said." He pointed to Betsy Sanders, one of the board members.

"That is so not true, and you know it, Ken," said Betsy. "Since I've been recording their conversations, it hasn't happened again."

"Wait," said Matthews. "You are recording what people say? And they are okay with this?"

"Beats me," said Betsy. "I haven't told them I'm doing it. It seemed easier that way."

"And we like simple meetings, without a lot of fuss, so we can get things done and go home," said Ken.

Matthews distinctly remembered that the board had said during the interview process that they liked having community members in attendance at the meetings. The board had assured him that they preferred over-communication to none at all, and that they had an effective communication system in place. There was no reason to change what was working.

During that meeting, Matthews learned that the board members often e-mailed school administrators at the campuses and at central office several times a day, asking for information so they could make informed decisions or put out the "tinier fires," as they called small issues.

The next day, Matthews met with his cabinet to tell them what the school board had discussed. The team members sitting at the conference table with their cups of coffee and bottled water looked a little surprised at being called in for a meeting, and they were more surprised that the superintendent had updates for them.

"How else will you know what's going on?" asked Matthews.

"We find out from others," said the special education director.

The director of Curriculum and Instruction spoke up: "If we need to know something, one of the board members emails us or calls us, and we act on that."

"Yeah, until another board member calls with a different directive. Then we have to change what we are doing," said the HR director.

Leonard Matthews knew he had to make some serious changes, and he had to make them fast. He wanted desperately to help so many of the Milford County students, but couldn't unless he streamlined one thing first.

Table 18.1 Other Information

DISTRICT OVERVIEW
About Milford County schools

	% White	% African American	% Hispanic	% Other
Student population	57	32	10	1
Student passing rate	76	40	54	1
Attendance rate	90	68	73	1
Graduation rate	88	73	70	1

Staffing (FTEs)

Teachers with 0–2 years' experience	47
Teachers with 3–5 years' experience	57
Teachers with 6–10 years' experience	42
Teachers with 11–15 years' experience	23
Teachers with 16–20 years' experience	15
Teachers with 20+ years' experience	7

Administrators

Administrators with 0–2 years' experience	1
Administrators with 3–5 years' experience	6
Administrators with 6–10 years' experience	2
Administrators with 11–15 years' experience	0
Administrators with 16–20 years' experience	0
Administrators with 20+ years' experience	0

Community Satisfaction Survey (1–10, with 10 being the highest)

Staffing	9.2
Finances	8.7
Operations	8.5
Student achievement	8.3
Professional development	6.2
Communication	3.7

PARTIAL LIST OF INTERVIEW QUESTIONS FOR
THE SUPERINTENDENT

1. What education and experiences have prepared you for this position?
2. What interests you about working in our school district?
3. What do you know about our district and community?
4. How well do you respond to supervision and criticism?
5. What do you know about the members of the school board?
6. How do you feel about moving to our community?
7. How would you want to communicate with the members of the school board?
8. How would you advise a school board member to respond if parents contact them directly about school issues?
9. Do you think the school board ought to evaluate itself? Why or why not?
10. How do you feel about school administrators and teachers attending school board meetings?
11. Describe your leadership style. What do you do for fun?
12. Is an employees' union an advantage or a disadvantage? Defend your answer.
13. How would you help us increase funding opportunities?
14. How would you assure that the district curriculum is aligned with state standards?
15. How do you feel about professional development for employees? What about for the school board?

ISSUE

Leonard Matthews is the new superintendent of schools in Milford County. Although he's excited to make a big difference in the lives of students and teachers, he discovers that the school board has been acting in ways that it shouldn't. In fact, in an attempt to communicate well among board members, the members have created a convoluted process that takes time away from the school employee's days when they have to stop what they are doing to answer yet other questions.

DILEMMA

At the first school board meeting, Matthews discovers that the attendance at the public meeting is sparse because the board makes it known that they do not want visitors at the meetings. In addition, the board routinely solicits information from the superintendent's cabinet and then gets the information incorrect even though responses were recorded (without the employee's knowledge).

In addition, the cabinet members used to learn through hearsay what the board's goals were or how meetings went. They had been told that their attendance was not necessary at the meetings.

Matthews finds out fast that before he can get to the business of teaching students, he has to take care of a pervasive problem first, beginning with the school board.

QUESTIONS

1. How the questions asked during the interview process could prepare Matthews for what he would face as the superintendent?
2. What is the one thing Matthews ought to work on first? Why?
3. What changes does Matthews need to make regarding school board meetings? Why? What can the superintendent do to streamline communication between himself, his cabinet, and the school board?
4. What is the problem with the school board requesting information individually from members of the superintendent's cabinet? Why?
5. Can the school board direct the members of the superintendent's cabinet? Why or why not?
6. How can Matthews get the community involved?

Chapter 19

Reasons Why

Suburban School District (17 elementary schools, 4 middle schools, 3 high schools)

Standards: Professional Community for Teachers and Staff, 7b; Professional Capacity of School Personnel, 6c

BACKGROUND

Leslie Stoller is the superintendent of Valley View School District, a large district set in the suburbs. She has been leading the district for several years. She is a resident of the community, and her children and grandchildren also attended Valley View schools.

Recently, there have been several suicides that have occurred in the community. Each suicide was committed by a teenager enrolled in the schools. At last month's counselors' meeting, the counselors reported that they have seen a substantial increase in the number of students who have been self-harming or thinking about self-harming. The interest has caused alarm among the counselors, who have to fill out extensive paper work of a suicidal threat.

The problem, according to the counselors, is not the paperwork itself but the time it takes to tick off all the boxes; it's time that could be spent with other students who also need help. When the counselors asked the students for the reasons why they are hurting themselves, the students say it is because of a TV series called *13 Reasons Why*. The series is based on a book by the same title.

At the recommendation of the student services director, Superintendent Stoller provided a one-hour training on how to recognize self-harming and suicidal ideations.

The superintendent thought it was also important to let the community know what's going on. The following letter was sent home with the students, posted on the district website, and printed in the community newspaper.

It didn't take long before people began discussing the issue and the letter itself. The school employees, the community, and even people beyond the district began discussing the series, the book, and the letter. Many of the discussions took place in social media forums, and these discussions sparked interest, concern, and even anger about a storyline that would exalt suicide.

Letter from the superintendent of schools:

Many of you know me as an ardent advocate of not only student achievement, but also of good health. My goal in our district has been to help students see the greatest achievement levels possible while making sure we also pay attention to their physical and mental health.

You may have heard in the news and through social media that our district has experienced three suicides in recent months. It is three too many deaths. We will never know why three of our promising students, one middle schooler and two high students, have decided to end their precious lives so soon.

However, many other students may be considering copying their peers' behavior. The counselors across the district report to me that they have seen a tremendous uptick in self-harming ideations. In these instances, students are cutting themselves, sometimes with knives and razor blades, sometimes with a broken CD shard. The reasons are twofold. In some cases, the resulting pain helps students forget about other problems and pains. In other cases, students are emulating what they have seen on television and at the movies.

Such is the case with the release of the Netflix series *13 Reasons Why*. This series glorifies suicide. As a parent and grandparent, I would hesitate allowing my children to watch it. If they were still able to view it, I would have honest and candid discussions with them about the dangers of self-abuse and the finality of suicide.

The National Association of Psychologists agrees with me—this is not a series for children, especially those who could be considered vulnerable to suggestion. Why any media outlet would broadcast such a thing is beyond me.

Our teachers and counselors recently have received additional professional development in the identification of self-harming and suicidal ideations. Please be aware that your children may be hiding these behaviors from you.

If you have further questions or concerns, you may contact the counselors and/or school administrators at your child's campus. In the meantime, please refer to the attached information from the National association of School Psychologists.

Attachment: (1) 3 pages
National Association of School Psychologists (2017) Release:

NASP

NATIONAL ASSOCIATION OF
School Psychologists

13 Reasons Why Netflix Series: Considerations for Educators

Schools have an important role in preventing youth suicide, and being aware of potential risk factors in students' lives is vital to this responsibility. The trending Netflix series *13 Reasons Why*, based on a young adult novel of the same name, is raising such concerns. The series revolves around 17-year-old Hannah Baker, who takes her own life and leaves behind audio recordings for 13 people who she says in some way were part of why she killed herself. Each tape recounts painful events in which one or more of the 13 individuals played a role.

Producers for the show say they hope the series can help those who may be struggling with thoughts of suicide. However, the series, which many teenagers are binge watching without adult guidance and support, is raising concerns from suicide prevention experts about the potential risks posed by the sensationalized treatment of youth suicide. The series graphically depicts a suicide death and addresses in wrenching detail a number of difficult topics, such a bullying, rape, drunk driving, and slut shaming. The series also highlights the consequences of teenagers witnessing assaults and bullying (i.e., bystanders) and not taking action to address the situation (e.g., not speaking out against the incident, not telling an adult about the incident).

Figure 19.1 *13 Reasons Why* Netflix Series: Considerations for Educators
Source: National Association of School Psychologists. (2017). *13 Reasons Why* Netflix Series: Considerations for Educators [handout]. Bethesda, MD.

CAUTIONS

We do not recommend that vulnerable youth, especially those who have any degree of suicidal ideation, watch this series. Its powerful storytelling may lead impressionable viewers to romanticize the choices made by the characters and/or develop revenge fantasies. They may easily identify with the experiences portrayed and recognize both the intentional and unintentional effects on the central character. Unfortunately, adult characters in the show, including the second school counselor who inadequately addresses Hannah's pleas for help, do not inspire a sense of trust or ability to help. Hannah's parents are also unaware of the events that lead her suicide death.

While many youth are resilient and capable of differentiating between a TV drama and real life, engaging in thoughtful conversations with them about the show is vital. Doing so presents an opportunity to help them process the issues addressed, consider the consequences of certain choices, and reinforce the message that **suicide is not a solution to problems** and that help is available. **This is particularly important for adolescents who are isolated, struggling, or vulnerable to suggestive images and storylines.** Research shows that exposure to another person's suicide, or to graphic or sensationalized accounts of death, can be one of the many risk factors that youth struggling with mental health conditions cite as a reason they contemplate or attempt suicide.

What the series does accurately convey is that there is no single cause of suicide. Indeed, there are likely as many different pathways to suicide as there are suicide deaths. However, the series does not emphasize that common among most suicide deaths is the presence of treatable mental illnesses. Suicide is **not** the simple consequence of stressors or coping challenges, but rather, it is most typically a combined result of treatable mental illnesses and overwhelming or intolerable stressors.

School psychologists and other school-employed mental health professionals can assist stakeholders (e.g., school administrators, parents, and teachers) to engage in supportive conversations with students as well as provide resources and offer expertise in preventing harmful behaviors.

Figure 19.2 *13 Reasons Why* Netflix Series: Considerations for Educators
Source: National Association of School Psychologists. (2017). *13 Reasons Why* Netflix Series: Considerations for Educators [handout]. Bethesda, MD.

GUIDANCE FOR EDUCATORS

1. While we do not recommend that all students view this series, it can be appreciated as an opportunity to better understand young people's experiences, thoughts, and feelings. Children and youth who view this series will need supportive adults to process it. Take this opportunity to both prevent the risk of harm and identify ongoing social and behavior problems in the school community that may need to be addressed.

2. Help students articulate their perceptions when viewing controversial content, such as *13 Reasons Why*. The difficult issues portrayed do occur in schools and communities, and it is important for adults to listen, take adolescents' concerns seriously, and be willing to offer to help.

3. Reinforce that school-employed mental health professionals are available to help. Emphasize that the behavior of the second counselor in the series is understood by virtually all school-employed mental health professionals as inappropriate. It is important that all school-employed mental health professionals receive training in suicide risk assessment.

4. Make sure parents, teachers, and students are aware of suicide risk warning signs. **Always take warning signs seriously, and never promise to keep them secret. Establish a confidential reporting mechanism for students.** Common signs include:
   - Suicide threats, both direct ("I am going to kill myself." "I need life to stop.") and indirect ("I need it to stop." "I wish I could fall asleep and never wake up."). Threats can be verbal or written, and they are often found in online postings.
   - Giving away prized possessions.
   - Preoccupation with death in conversation, writing, drawing, and social media.
   - Changes in behavior, appearance/hygiene, thoughts, and/or feelings. This can include someone who is typically sad who suddenly becomes extremely happy.
   - Emotional distress.

Figure 19.3 *13 Reasons Why* Netflix Series: Considerations for Educators
Source: National Association of School Psychologists. (2017). *13 Reasons Why* Netflix Series: Considerations for Educators [handout]. Bethesda, MD.

6. Separate myths and facts.
   - **MYTH:** Talking about suicide will make someone want to commit suicide who has never thought about it before. **FACT:** There is no evidence to suggest that talking about suicide plants the idea. Talking with your friend about how they feel and letting them know that you care about them is important. This is the first step in getting your friend help.
   - **MYTH:** People who struggle with depression or other mental illness are just weak. **FACT:** Depression and other mental illnesses are serious health conditions and are treatable.
   - **MYTH:** People who talk about suicide won't really do it. **FACT:** People, particularly young people who are thinking about suicide, typically demonstrate warning signs. Always take these warning signs seriously.

7. **Never leave the person alone; seek out a trusted adult immediately.** School-employed mental health professionals like your school psychologist are trusted sources of help.

8. Work with other students and the adults in the school if you want to develop a memorial for someone who has committed suicide. Although decorating a student's locker, creating a memorial social media page, or other similar activities are quick ways to remember the student who has died, they may influence others to imitate or have thoughts of wanting to die as well. It is recommended that schools develop memorial activities that encourage hope and promote positive outcomes for others (e.g., suicide prevention programs).

Figure 19.4 *13 Reasons Why* Netflix Series: Considerations for Educators
Source: National Association of School Psychologists. (2017). *13 Reasons Why* Netflix Series: Considerations for Educators [handout]. Bethesda, MD.

5. Students who feel suicidal are not likely to seek help directly; however, parents, school personnel, and peers can recognize the warning signs and take immediate action to keep the youth safe. When a student gives signs that they may be considering suicide, take the following actions.
   • Remain calm, be nonjudgmental, and listen. Strive to understand the intolerable emotional pain that has resulted in suicidal thoughts.
   • Avoid statements that might be perceived as minimizing the student's emotional pain (e.g., "You need to move on." or "You should get over it.").
   • Ask the student **directly** if they are thinking about suicide (i.e., "Are you thinking of suicide?").
   • Focus on your concern for their well-being and avoid being accusatory.
   • Reassure the student that there is help and they will not feel like this forever.
   • Provide constant supervision. **Do not leave the student alone.**
   • Without putting yourself in danger, remove means for self-harm, including any weapons the person might find.
   • **Get help.** Never agree to keep a student's suicidal thoughts a secret. Instead, school staff should take the student to a school-employed mental health professional. Parents should seek help from school or community mental health resources. Students should tell an appropriate caregiving adult, such as a school psychologist, administrator, parent, or teacher.
6. School or district officials should determine how to handle memorials after a student has died. Promote memorials that benefit others (e.g., donations for a suicide prevention program) and activities that foster a sense of hope and encourage positive action. The memorial should not glorify, highlight, or accentuate the individual's death. It may lead to imitative behaviors or a suicide contagion (Brock et al., 2016).
7. Reinforcing resiliency factors can lessen the potential of risk factors that lead to suicidal ideation and behaviors. Once a child or adolescent is considered at risk, schools, families, and friends should work to build these factors in and around the youth.
   • Family support and cohesion, including good communication.
   • Peer support and close social networks.
   • School and community connectedness.

Figure 19.5 *13 Reasons Why* Netflix Series: Considerations for Educators
Source: National Association of School Psychologists. (2017). *13 Reasons Why* Netflix Series: Considerations for Educators [handout]. Bethesda, MD.

Social Media Comments and Posts:

• Schools are refusing to report how serious this problem is—they are pushing bad behavior under the carpet just so they look good. Send out a letter and wash your hands of it. I say you are washing your hands in the blood of our children.
• Art imitates life; life imitates art.
• I'd paddle my child if he did that.
• It's not a TV show that makes children want to kill themselves—it's boring classes and excessive high-stakes testing.
• School leaders need to stop bullying now.
• Until you stop the bullying, you won't stop the emotional stress.
• The issues are with poorly raised children. The problem is a PC culture that won't step in and redirect children—or adults.
• It's the school's fault for not addressing the problem to begin with.
• Sure, blame school for everything. Where is parent and personal responsibility?
• The series and the book should be banned. Who lets students see this stuff?

Read these helpful points from SAVE.org and the JED Foundation to further understand how *13 Reasons Why* dramatizes situations and the realities of suicide. See Save a Friend: Tips for Teens to Prevent Suicide for additional information.

ADDITIONAL RESOURCES

- Center for Disease Control Suicide Datasheet
- SAMHSA Prevention Suicide: A Toolkit for High Schools
- Suicide Prevention Resource Center, After a Suicide: Toolkit for Schools
- Memorials: Special Considerations for Memorializing an Incident

WEBSITES

- National Association of School Psychologists, www.nasponline.org
- American Association of Suicidology, www.suicidology.org
- Suicide Awareness Voices of Education, www.save.org
- American Foundation for Suicide Prevention, https://afsp.org/
- www.stopbullying.gov
- Rape, Abuse & Incest National Network, www.rainn.org

REFERENCES

Brock, S. E., Nickerson, A. B., Louvar Reeves, M. A., Conolly, S., Jimerson, S., Pesce, R, & Lazarro, B. (2016). *School crisis prevention and intervention: The PREP_aRE model* (2nd ed.). Bethesda, MD: National Association of School Psychologists.

Contributors: Christina Conolly, Kathy Cowan, Peter Faustino, Ben Fernandez, Stephen Brock, Melissa Reeves, Rich Lieberman

Document may be adapted or excerpted with proper acknowledgement. Please cite as:

National Association of School Psychologists. (2017). *13 Reasons Why Netflix series: Considerations for educators* [handout]. Bethesda, MD: Author.

Figure 19.6 *13 Reasons Why* Netflix Series: Considerations for Educators
Source: National Association of School Psychologists. (2017). *13 Reasons Why* Netflix Series: Considerations for Educators [handout]. Bethesda, MD.

- The problem is that health care often doesn't include mental health assistance—and look where it's gotten us now.
- Schools need to teach. Teach the basics, let mommy and daddy step in and be parents. Stop coddling children. They'll never grow up.

ISSUE

A recent TV series has sparked interest in self-harming and suicide among the students at every level. As a result, there have been three recent teenage suicides in the district, and a considerable number of students are practicing self-harming behaviors, namely cutting.

In response to the popularity of the show and the increase in abusive behaviors, the superintendent wrote a letter for the parents about the situation. The superintendent strongly encouraged parents to not let their children view the series because of its damaging effects.

The letter has sparked a firestorm of publicity and comments.

DILEMMA

Superintendent Stoller addressed a health challenge in her district by sending a letter home to all of the parents about abusive student behaviors.

The letter went viral, traveling far outside the school district community. Unfortunately there was some questionable content in the letter, including detailed descriptions and a personal judgment about the wisdom of televising the series and allowing children to watch it.

QUESTIONS

1. What was good about the superintendent's letter to the community? Why? What should *not* be in the letter? Why?
2. Should the NASP article have been printed and included? Why? What's a better way to include their statement?
3. What sort of intervention training should the district provide to the employees? At what point, if any, should the district include parents?
4. How serious should the school district take the threat of copycat behaviors among the students? Why?
5. After viewing the series and monitoring social media comments, the administrators may have other issues to consider addressing. What are they?
6. Should the English teachers teach the book in class? Why or why not?

Chapter 20

My Lawyer Will Be in Touch

Urban School District (27 elementary schools, 9 middle schools, 4 high schools)

Standards: Community of Care and Support of Students, 5e; Meaningful Engagement of Families and Community, 8a, h

BACKGROUND

After meeting with the high school principal and the superintendent of schools, Mrs. Brown was still unhappy. Her son Antwan would be graduating this year, and she was convinced he was not ready to leave school and enter the workforce.

Her rationale for her decision included the fact that Antwan could not read on grade level, nor could he perform basic math calculations. He was unprepared.

To make matters worse, the Danforth high school principal was part of the problem instead of the solution. Over the course of Antwan's education, Mrs. Brown's son had been suspended from school for more than 200 days. She argued that the school kicked him out for more than a year. No wonder he was so far behind!

According to Mrs. Brown, her son was denied his right to literacy.

She tried to explain this to Mrs. Bowen, the current superintendent of schools. Mrs. Brown met with Mrs. Bowen at the superintendent office. Although she had been very concerned about whether tax payer money was being used to decorate the administrative office or supply guest beverages, Mrs. Brown wanted taxpayer money in order to hire a private tutor for Antwan.

Mrs. Bowen felt certain when Mrs. Brown left the office after their conversation, the mother wouldn't let the matter lie. She would pursue this track no matter what. The superintendent didn't feel comfortable offering a private tutor to catch Antwan up, even though he had been suspended 211 days from school over the past seven years. Mrs. Brown had gathered the signatures of some 300 parents who felt the same way: the schools in the districts were targeting students of color, preventing them from getting the education they deserved.

The superintendent had been savvy enough to seek district legal counsel regarding the matter. The school attorney advised Mrs. Allen, the high school principal, that she should make tutoring available at the school, like she would for any other student, but that she should not offer the services of a private tutor for Antwan. The child had misbehaved, and he had not followed the student code of conduct set forth by the district. The mother should have been involved in the child's education long before his senior year of school. To offer him specialized services when he was not even in a special program would set a poor precedent.

Mrs. Brown signed up to speak at the next school board meeting. She held nearly 400 signatures in her hand while she passionately spoke about how students were being racially discriminated against. "This is not just about Antwan," she said. "This is about all students of color. All students who are immediately suspended from school even though their white peers are given a verbal reprimand and sent back to class. Which students do you think perform better on state assessments? Which read better? Understand more math? THE ONES WHO ARE IN SCHOOL!"

She received thunderous applause, and it was obvious that many of the parents agreed with her. The school board agreed to make Mrs. Brown's concerns an agenda item at their next meeting.

Two weeks later, the board discussed the situation regarding students who were suspended from school and prevented from continuing their instruction. While the board members felt there may be "something to" Mrs. Brown's claim, they also felt that the district was doing pretty well in educating most children. All anyone had to do was compare the scores to those of other districts in the city and across the state.

Mrs. Brown shook her head. They still didn't get it. There were plenty of students just like Antwan who had not been able to acquire the necessary literacy skills because they had been discriminated against when it came to discipline management.

The only thing left to do would be to file a class action complaint. Her team of attorneys were ready to file suit in the U.S. Court of Appeals on the grounds that the school leaders, the superintendent, the school board members, the state education director, and even the governor were indifferent and complacent about the whole matter of literacy for students of color.

Students were graduating without even being able to read on or near-grade level. They didn't have the reading skills to pass standardized assessments, and they didn't have the necessary literacy skills for gainful employment.

"We just want our kids to have what's rightfully theirs," said Mrs. Brown. This is the data that was compiled for the meeting:

Use this key for all data tables:

AA = African American
H = Hispanic
W = White
AI = American Indian
PI = Pacific Islander
SE = Special Education
ECO DIS = Economically disadvantaged
ELL = English Language Learner

Table 20.1 Academic Data from State Assessment; the Identified School Is Danforth High

Reading	Campuses				Race						Populations		
	State	City	District	School	AA	H	W	AI	A	PI	SE	ECO DIS	ELL
9th	82	75	81	88	64	75	95	–	100	–	87	85	78
10th	85	74	86	91	67	71	94	–	100	–	82	81	81
11th	87	71	85	92	68	76	97	–	100	–	74	85	89
12th	85	78	80	89	65	72	93	–	100	–	72	83	91

Table 20.2 High School Math Scores by Race

Math	Campuses				Race						Populations		
	State	City	District	School	AA	H	W	AI	A	PI	SE	ECO DIS	ELL
9th	73	67	75	73	45	64	77	–	95	–	78	75	54
10th	75	65	76	75	57	68	78	–	100	–	74	69	62
11th	71	69	73	76	53	68	76	–	100	–	72	62	65
12th	74	70	77	74	51	65	76	–	100	–	75	60	71

Table 20.3 Average Percentile in Reading across Four District High Schools

Reading	Race						Populations		
	AA	H	W	AI	A	PI	SE	ECO DIS	ELL
9th	17	43	86	–	100	–	87	85	78
10th	28	42	88	–	100	–	82	81	81
11th	22	37	90	–	100	–	74	85	89
12th	24	31	91	–	100	–	72	83	91

Table 20.4 Average Percentile in Reading at Danforth High School

Reading	Race						Populations		
	AA	H	W	AI	A	PI	SE	ECO DIS	ELL
9th	17	43	86	–	100	–	42	40	48
10th	28	42	88	–	100	–	39	37	40
11th	22	37	90	–	100	–	25	34	42
12th	24	31	91	–	100	–	27	27	45

Table 20.5 Average Percentile in Math across Four District High Schools

Math	Race						Populations		
	AA	H	W	AI	A	PI	SE	ECO DIS	ELL
9th	22	52	85	–	98	–	44	39	54
10th	32	56	88	–	100	–	42	37	62
11th	27	54	86	–	100	–	47	42	61
12th	21	53	87	–	100	–	43	54	58

Table 20.6 Average Percentile in Reading at Danforth High School

Math	Race						Populations		
	AA	H	W	AI	A	PI	SE	ECO DIS	ELL
9th	14	45	82	–	100	–	42	35	52
10th	12	48	78	–	100	–	40	31	58
11th	15	54	77	–	100	–	43	39	57
12th	9	50	71	–	100	–	38	51	65

ISSUE

Mrs. Brown has not given up on helping her son Antwan. She has gathered even more signatures on her petition, requesting that the school district provide intervention for Antwan and others like him because they have been suspended more often due to the color of their skin.

As a result, these students have missed a considerable amount of school, and the parents ascertain that the students missed critical learning blocks that are the foundation of literacy in reading and in mathematics. Even percentile scores show a great disparity between white students and students of color.

DILEMMA

Mrs. Brown, as unsatisfied as ever, went to the board meeting to speak her mind. During her three minutes of public comments, she presented her case and requested that the school board explore whether she was right—inequitable discipline practices are preventing students of color from getting the education they deserve.

The board asked Mrs. Bowen, "Why didn't you tell us about this before now?"

When the school board reviewed the claims, they quickly pointed out that although Danforth High School could use some work, the district had performed just as well as other districts in the city, if not across the state.

Now Mrs. Brown wanted to file a class action complaint on the behalf of her son and other children like him.

QUESTIONS

1. What would you have done with the legal advice the attorney gave the superintendent? Why? How should the advice be documented?
2. What other documentation should be gathered on the behalf of the district? Why?
3. Why should the superintendent keep the school board informed of possible volatile situations and impending lawsuits?
4. Can the parent file a class action complaint against the individuals and the organizations?
5. What's the problem with having lawsuits in a school district?

Chapter 21

Just between Us

Rural School District (6 elementary schools, 2 middle schools, 1 high school) Standards: Ethics and Professional Norms, 2a, b; Operations and Management, 9k, l

BACKGROUND

The Mountain Laurel School District hired Ray Rousch as their superintendent.

Mr. Rousch had to convince his wife that this was the right opportunity for their family. It meant leaving the city and working in a much tinier community where there weren't a whole lot of social activities. Fortunately, Mrs. Rousch worked as a telecommuter; she could continue her job from anywhere. She agreed to make the move with her husband.

As a first-time superintendent, Ray was excited about his new position. It meant an opportunity to lead an entire district to new levels of achievement. The district had just nine schools. It was small, but it seemed like each school was committed to student success. Their challenge was that they had neither the technology they needed to keep up with larger districts and the world online, nor did they have the funds for immediate upgrades.

Like other districts across the state, the Mountain Laurel District had seen huge cutbacks from both federal and state funding, and it didn't seem like the residents in the community could handle another tax increase. Mr. Rousch wanted to provide the students with as much up-to-date technology as possible. He saw interactive technology as a way students could connect with the world, and teachers could participate in just-in-time learning opportunities. With the right technology, the students and employees wouldn't be stuck in their tiny, out-of-the-way rural location.

Because of the constricted budget, Mr. Rousch determined that seeking additional funds through the services of a grant writer would be the way to go. The salary for the right employee would more than pay for itself. All the superintendent had to do was convince the school board, and he was certain he could do that.

Even better, he knew the right person for the job, too. Marcus Daly was a young millennial more than familiar with technology. He was well connected with other tech types, and although he had written only one other grant in his life—for the city's Boys' and Girls' Club—it had been funded. Mr. Rousch had met Marcus in a coffee shop at the airport.

They were each flying out in different directions, but hit it off immediately and exchanged contact information.

Marcus was just the person he needed in the grant writing position. It would be good to have him close by, as well, because they could see each other more often without having to drive several hours away to the city.

Mr. Rousch intended to make the request at the March Special Board Meeting. The tax rate would be on the agenda, and it was the perfect time to get approval for a position that could bring money into the district. If he got the position and the employee approved, Marcus would have a jump-start on the next academic year to get a couple of grants funded.

Normally Mr. Rousch would have revealed his connection to an employee to be sure there was no appearance of nepotism. But Marcus Daly was not related to him, and Ray saw no reason to reveal his secret relationship. No one ever had to find out.

The school board meeting went off without a hitch. The board looked relieved that Mr. Rousch has a solution for tough economic times, and they approved the new FTE as well as Ray's recommendation that they hire Marcus Daly. The board agreed unanimously that the grants officer should report directly to the superintendent. There was a bit of a sticking point on the stipends for Ray, but there were times he would have to put in prolonged hours well beyond the workweek, especially when approaching deadlines for competitive grants. Marcus may even need to hire outside assistance during those times.

Marcus had just gotten his first request for proposal sent out when Mr. Rousch walked into the grant officer's office and closed the door.

"I think you'd better pack your bags," said the superintendent.

"What?" asked Marcus. "I thought you liked my work. I thought you liked me."

"I do," said the superintendent. "There's a conference next week that I'd like you to go to. I think I may even stop in for a day or two."

When Rousch and Daly returned from the conference, there was a noticeable difference in the attitude of many of the employees. They seemed aloof. Marcus noticed the change first.

"What's up with everyone around here?" he asked Ray when the two of them happened to be in the admin kitchen at the same time getting coffee.

"Beats me," said Mr. Rousch.

It wasn't long before the superintendent found out just what the problem was. Apparently, someone from the community discovered the relationship and even claimed to have proof that it existed.

If that were the case, there could be some real challenges ahead.

Review the following pieces of information:

SCHOOL BOARD AGENDA (from the meeting where Marcus was hired 473 views)

NOTICE OF SPECIAL MEETING

BOARD OF TRUSTEES

MOUNTAIN LAUREL SCHOOL DISTRICT

555 Crestview @ the Administration Building

March 22

6:00 p.m.

THE BOARD MAY CHOOSE TO DISCUSS ITEMS IN ANY ORDER.

I.   **Call Meeting to Order**
II.   **Declare Quorum**
III. **Approval of Minutes**
      A. Regular Called Meeting March 16
IV.   **Superintendent's Report**
      A. Recognition of District for Food Bank support
      B. Tax collection update
V.   **Discussion Items**
VI.   **Public Comments**
VII. **Business and Finance**
VIII. **Human Resources**
      A. Reclassification of position/Grants Officer
      B. Stipends for reclassification
IX.   **Into Executive Session**

Figure 21.1 Notice of Special Meeting

SOCIAL MEDIA POST

Guess which district leader was seen holding hands with the district grants officer?

Figure 21.2 Social Media Post

OMG. Is that Marcus? I'd know him anywhere.
Who is he with?
He?
Marcus.
The supe.
Our superintendent has a lover?
Wait, the superintendent is GAY? I thought he was married.

TEXTS FROM THE SUPERINTENDENT'S DISTRICT MOBILE PHONE

Marcus—Check your page. They know.
Ray—Who knows?
Marcus—By now, everyone. Someone posted a picture of us.
Ray—WTH?
Marcus—I know.

Ray—I don't want my wife to know.
Marcus—Dude, are you kidding?
Ray—No I'm not. She has no idea.

ISSUE

Mr. Rousch is a new superintendent who wants to move the district forward in the area of technology. The community is not able to take on an increased tax burden, so Mr. Rousch has been looking for alternative ways to raise much-needed funds for technology. He was instrumental in getting a new position approved, and he also had someone appointed to the job.

The new grants officer jumped in and got to work immediately, sending out his first RFP rather quickly. To celebrate, Mr. Rousch sent Daly to a conference, where he later joined the grants officer.

While away at the conference, someone had seen the two lovers and photographed them. They also posted the picture in social media.

DILEMMA

Mr. Rousch hired Marcus Daly through unscrupulous practices. Not only did he have someone picked out for the position without even posting the position internally or interviewing candidates, but he also forced Daly's application and recommended that he be hired.

Mr. Rousch failed to reveal that he was in a relationship with the potential employee. The relationship was discovered while the two of them were at the same conference. Another district employee happened to be at the same conference and took a picture of them. Then she posted the proof on a social media page.

Mrs. Rousch was also unaware of the relationship. Now she, along with everyone else, knows that her husband is gay.

QUESTIONS

1. Is hiring Marcus Daly a case of nepotism? Why or why not?
2. How has the superintendent set himself up for a sexual harassment claim?
3. Whom should the grants officer have reported to? Why?
4. What's the bigger issue? Hiring someone with whom you are having a relationship or being gay in a small rural community? Why?
5. How would you advise Ray Rousch to handle questions and concerns from the community?

Chapter 22

I Got Mine

Suburban School District (16 elementary schools, 4 middle schools, 2 high schools)
Standards: Ethics and Professional Norms, 2a, b; Operations and Management, 9k, l

BACKGROUND

Susan Neese was a powerhouse of the superintendent. She had been in the Golden Acres School District for eight years, she was completing her fourth contract as the district leader. When she first came to the school district, she had agreed to the one-year temporary contract offered to her by the school board. The school board like her so much that each of the subsequent contracts was for three years a piece, and they always ended with an option to renew.

Mrs. Neese had two years left in the sports contract. She didn't want to tell the school board about this, but this was probably going to be her last two years in education. Also she was great at what she did; the job was stressful and demanding. Mrs. Neese was ready for a break. She knew just rushing would take it too. The cost of living in Central America was cheap, and the thoughts of living in Belize were looking better and better with each teacher contract negotiation and student sporting event that Mrs. Neese found herself a part of.

Best of all, Mrs. Neese would have plenty of money to live on for the rest of her life. Being a superintendent at the Golden Acres School District not only had been lucrative—she was the highest-paid superintendent in the state—but also she had made a few extra dollars on the side, thanks to the way her contract had been written and interpreted, and of course, her own ability to pad her regular salary with additional stipends.

There have been rocky times, of course, like the year that Mrs. Neese introduced a new reading program and a new math program at the same time. The initiative required the addition of reading and math specialists at every campus. Although the specialized certification cost the district an additional $8.3 million in salaries alone the first year of implementation, the academic achievement of the students was worth every dollar and every parent complaint. The school board agreed to continue the program every year after that.

"You've got to spend the money to make money," said Mrs. Neese. She pointed out that because the achievement rates were so high in the district, more people wanted to move within their district boundaries to take advantage of the good schools. In turn, property values skyrocketed, as did taxes. It was a win–win situation for everyone.

The other big challenge Mrs. Neese faced was the school bond she got passed. Building the new and much-needed elementary school this year was going to cost the district $25 million. The cost couldn't be helped; schools weren't cheap. Even elementary schools commanded a big price, especially with all the extras. The superintendent has insisted on adding a premiere playscape for the students. By the time all of the components have been selected, the area level marked off and filled with rubber chips rather than pebbles, the cost of the playscape came to $196,000. Mrs. Neese knew that there was no way the community could raise the money necessary for the playground, so she rolled cost into the bond.

There were a few other things the district had taken care of and she included those costs into the bond as well. For example, the state passed a law that all classrooms and corridors must be fitted with cameras so that any incidents of bad behavior could be reviewed on camera and documented visually. Like many state mandates, this was an unfunded state initiative, and the school district had to come up with cameras and monitoring systems for 22 schools. The resulting $2.2 million was added to the bond request.

In addition, several of the district's vehicles needed to be replaced. The superintendent-owned district vehicle was three years old, and it certainly needed to be replaced. The SUV had 150,000 miles on it, and was frequently in the shop for routine maintenance and occasional repair. Of course, during those days Mrs. Neese drove her personal vehicle on district business and charged the mileage to the district.

At any rate, by the time the superintendent added special programs and perks to the bond request, the amount being requested went well beyond $25 million. The bond package was $53.4 million.

"You've got to spend the money to make money," said Mrs. Neese.

That wasn't the worst part.

The school board and the community might have been able to tolerate the $50+ million indebtedness they would be facing, but the superintendent opted for long-term bond financing. By electing to have a longer payout, the district would own nine times the amount they were financing, or $465 million in principal and interest. It would take several generations to pay off the bond, and surely there would be other needs along the way.

Members of the school board were furious when they found out that Mrs. Neese had signed the agreement for the financing without their approval.

It was supposed to have been a discussion item at the next school board meeting.

Mrs. Neese smiled and said, "I wanted to surprise you."

The school board surprised Mrs. Neese. At the beginning of the meeting, they placed her on administrative leave pending an investigation.

There was no doubt that Mrs. Neese understood curriculum and instruction. She also knew how to get student services to step up to really help students. Apparently she had a good handle on budgeting and finance. The problem was that she always looked out for herself, too well.

The school board discovered that in addition to the superintendent's base salary and benefits, she had also been taking vacation payouts, she had unreported vacation days, she awarded herself authorized raises and bonuses, and she collected checks for longevity pay. These are some of the documents the investigation uncovered:

Table 22.1 Base Salary and Benefits

	Benefits (Health Insurance/ Retirement)	Total
Year 1—$299,000	$59,800	$358,800
Year 2—$325,000	$65,000	$390,000
Year 3—$352,000	$70,400	$422,400
Year 4—$378,000	$76,500	$453,600
Year 5—$399,000	$79,800	$478,800
Year 6—$435,000	$87,000	$522,000
Year 7—$475,000	$95,000	$570,000

Table 22.2 Vacation Payouts
(Mrs. Neese reported her vacation days as unused. She had to attend to district business on her vacation time.)

Year and Daily Rate	Vacation Days Not Used	Total
Year 1—$1,370	2	$2,740
Year 2—$1,489	4	$5,956
Year 3—$1,612	5	$8,060
Year 4—$1,731	3	$5,193
Year 5—$1,827	11	$20,097
Year 6—$1,992	22	$43,824
Year 7—$2,176	16	$34816
	63	$120,686

Table 22.3 Unreported Vacation Days

Base Salary	Total
Year 1	1
Year 2	4
Year 3	3
Year 4	6
Year 5	12
Year 6	10
Year 7	8

Table 22.4 Raises and Bonuses
(Mrs. Neese received these amounts as separate checks in addition to her regular pay.)

Year of Employment	Raises and Bonuses
Year 1	$6,000
Year 2	$6,500
Year 3	$7,000
Year 4	$7,650
Year 5	$8,000
Year 6	$8,700
Year 7	$9,500
Total	$53,350

Table 22.5 Longevity Pay

Year of Employment	Stipend
Year 1	0
Year 2	$10,000
Year 3	$10,000
Year 4	$10,000
Year 5	$15,000
Year 6	$15,000
Year 7	$15,000
Total	$75,000

ISSUE

Mrs. Neese is an experienced superintendent with considerable financial savvy. She has seen to it that she has always been financially rewarded for her services. She has also kept meticulous records of every district business that has interrupted her vacation time. If someone called her regarding district business while she was on vacation, she counted that day as lost vacation time, claiming that she couldn't stop thinking about the district after the call.

Mrs. Neese recently signed on a bond contract the school board wanted to discuss before agreeing to. The bond would be paid off at a rate nine times greater than the amount borrowed.

Mrs. Neese's response was, "You have to spend money to make money."

DILEMMA

Mrs. Neese has been a talented superintendent. Under her leadership, the schools in the district have experienced great success, and the students have seen remarkable achievement. However, this kind of success has not been without a cost to the community. Not only has Mrs. Neese implemented expensive programs with long lives and great costs, but she has also rewarded herself handsomely for her work.

In addition to being the highest-paid superintendent of schools in the state, she has received at least a quarter million dollars in additional bonuses and stipends. Now the school may even have to buy out her contract, and the school board is concerned about how much this superintendent has cost them.

QUESTIONS

1. What's wrong with adding additional projects to the bond package for financing?
2. What was wrong with the long-term payment plan Mrs. Neese approved? Why was it a problem?
3. Should Mrs. Neese have signed the bond contract or waited for the school board? Why?
4. Mrs. Neese awarded herself at least an additional $250,000 during her employment as the superintendent. Was this a problem? Why or why not?
5. Can a superintendent be reimbursed for vacation days used by the district? Why or why not?

Chapter 23

What's for Lunch?

Suburban School District
Standards: Equity and Cultural Responsiveness, 3a; Meaningful Engagement of Families and Community, 8i; Operations and Management, 9c

BACKGROUND

Salvador Estrada was the superintendent of schools in an urban school district. Many of the students qualified for Title I services, and that meant that they were eligible for free and reduced meals at school as well.

The school lunch program had become increasingly more difficult to manage and operate with each passing year. New food standards made it virtually impossible to provide healthier food options at a reasonable price. Very often, it seemed that the cost preparing the meals exceeded what the district received in reimbursements.

Not only that, but the district was also expected to provide a hot meal substitution for any students with special dietary needs because of their health or because of their religion. The superintendent wished for the days of the past when all you have to do is hand out the peanut butter and jelly sandwich if the student couldn't eat what was being served.

He had seen what was being served in the cafeterias, and it had become less than appetizing. To make matters worse, the portions were smaller too, thanks to federal guidelines that had shrunk the serving sizes and calorie counts.

When the new program had been implemented, Superintendent Estrada heard numerous complaints that there was not enough food for students to eat, and students were simply starving while they waited for the next meal. Hungry students couldn't have second portions, and the firsts were skimpy

113

portions. That translated to headaches and hunger pangs that prevented students from concentrating in the classroom. To make matters worse, the school is no longer allowed to provide snacks for students after school during tutorials. They couldn't even provide snacks during instruction.

Students still threw away plenty of food. They dumped tray after tray of food, complaining about how tasteless it was. The superintendent had read somewhere that American students throw away $1.2 billion worth of food each year.

The whole school lunch program was problematic, and the superintendent was beginning to feel as though it wasn't worth the effort. He knew his heart, however, that the program really did help some of the students.

That's why he set up an Angel Fund to make sure that none of the children in his district ever went hungry if they truly wanted a meal. Employees could donate to the Angel Fund to provide meals for children whose parents otherwise could not afford to buy school lunch if their child did not qualify for Title I services or if a child simply forgot his lunch money. The superintendent himself donated hundred dollars a month to the fund.

Each month, the cafeteria manager had to submit the month's menu for both breakfast and lunch. A nutritionist reviewed the menu and made suggestions for improvements that had to be met. If the district failed to comply with state and federal laws regarding the school lunch program, the district would lose funding and have to repay any monies that it had received. The district also had to provide an equitable alternative to the meal being served. That meant that if the child could not eat the hotdogs that were being served, he or she still had to have access to a hot lunch, not a cold sandwich.

The superintendent wished that he could spend more time working on the instruction with the campus leaders, but it seemed bad there was always something to take care of with the school lunch program.

Today was no different. These are the communications Superintendent Estrada received:

LETTER TO THE SUPERINTENDENT

Dear Superintendent Estrada:

Your district has been chosen for an audit of your food services program.

We have noticed in the last six months period that your menus must frequently be revised to meet state and federal nutrition standards. Furthermore we have received a complaint that several of the cafeterias in your school district refused to provide an alternative hot meal for those students needing it.

We will be in your district the last week this month, and would initially like to meet with you and your student services director. We will then visit each of the cafeterias in your school district, and we will interview employees, students, and parents about current practices.

If you have any questions, don't hesitate to call my office.

Best regards,

Aman Abed

VOICE MAIL MESSAGE 1

I am calling to let you know that my children were once again served break-fast tacos at school. Not only do we not eat breakfast tacos in my culture, but we also are forbidden to eat bacon. It is unclean. This is the fourth time this year my children have gone without breakfast because they could not eat the food that was being served. The next time it happens I'm getting a lawyer.

VOICE MAIL MESSAGE 2

I just wanted to call and leave a quick message saying how wonderful Principal Bob Owens is. Last week he came to our apartment, with a variety of food left over from some of the school lunches. It was the only foods we had to eat all week. That's because I got laid off and didn't have money for the rent and for food. Even though what Mr. Owens brought us was leftover, it filled our bellies and kept going. He's a wonderful person and I thought you should know.

VOICE MAIL MESSAGE 3

I am a parent of one of your high school students, and today, against my wishes, I ate lunch with my daughter in her school cafeteria. I was dreading the experience because I remembered what my school lunches were like—horrible. First I must say I was pleasantly surprised. The green beans were especially delicious because of the pieces of real bacon in them. Good job to you and the cafeteria staff!

ISSUE

The school lunch program in the urban school district where Salvador Estrada is the superintendent is falling apart. The program barely makes enough money to break even, thanks to new regulations that seem to fail to meet student needs. The students are often hungry because they do not like the food, and there is not enough of it. The children complain after lunch that they are still hungry.

The district has not always provided comparable lunch alternatives, and some of the parents have complained. They have complained enough that the state is now looking into the matter.

DILEMMA

Superintendent Estrada faces several problems. The cafeteria menus released each month rarely need approval and must be redrafted to be in line with state and federal guidelines.

In addition, several of the cafeterias routinely serve foods that some students are not allowed to eat because of their religious practices. The breakfast and lunch items prepared by the cafeteria are not on the menu submitted to the state; the cafeteria staff preferred cooking these items on their own.

Finally, the superintendent learned from one of the parents and the community that one of his principals routinely delivers leftovers from the school cafeteria to the needy families in the community.

QUESTIONS

1. What is the biggest problem that Superintendent Estrada faces? Why?
2. Should Superintendent Estrada do away with the school lunch program altogether? Why or why not?
3. What can Superintendent Estrada do to convince the school nutritionist to prepare menus aligned to state and federal guidelines?
4. What should the superintendent do about bacon appearing in the food choices? Should he ban breakfast tacos?
5. What should the superintendent do about Principal Owens?

Chapter 24

Secrecy Is the Best Plan

Urban School District
Standards: Meaningful Engagement of Families and Community, 8a, b, c;
 Operations and Management, 9h

BACKGROUND

Cypress Creek School District was ready to hire a new superintendent. With their former superintendent retiring, it was time to bring the new superintendent on board. Several of the school board members wanted to have a short transition where the outgoing superintendent could help the incoming superintendent.

Fortunately, the school board has narrowed their choices down to two candidates.

The first candidate, Jackie Black, earned her doctorate in educational leadership, and she had considerable expertise in using big data and managing disruptive chaos. Her credentials were impressive because she was also a certified project planner. She had originally entered the workforce as a structural engineer but decided her calling was in education. She particularly enjoyed and excelled at planning initiatives and strategies, recommending and executing budgets, and meeting impressively big goals and objectives.

The school board loved her. They thought she was exactly what the school district needed.

The second candidate, Stewart Jefferson, got his beginning education by working as a second grade teacher. From there he became a grade-level chair, and an assistant principal. He quickly worked his way up to elementary school principal, and then he moved on to the secondary levels, where he continued to work closely with teachers and students. Community members wherever he had worked adored him. He was communicative, transparent, and well liked. His strengths included curriculum and instruction, as well as creating collaborative relationships.

The school board planned to make their decision about the new superintendent at the board meeting on the 15th of the month. The only problem was that the retiring superintendent once again forgot to prepare the agenda for the meeting. The superintendent needed to give it to his administrative assistant. The Friday before the meeting, no public notice had been given regarding the upcoming school board meeting or what the seven-member board would be discussing.

That did not stop the school board from meeting.

At the meeting, one of the members made a motion that the board accept Jackie Black as the new superintendent of schools for Cypress Creek School District. No one seconded the motion, but immediately three other board members agreed that Jackie was the best choice for the school district's needs. Two of the other board members said nothing. The final board member raised his hand.

"Excuse me?" he asked. "Shouldn't we be hearing public comments on this or something? Doesn't it seem weird to you that there's no one else here for this meeting?"

His concern was quickly dismissed.

The school board president called Jackie Black on the phone and congratulated her for being the new superintendent of schools. He also asked her to write a short press release announcing her of employment. "I'd like to get this in the newspaper as quickly as possible," said the president.

When the community learned of the announcement, many of the members were outraged. There had been a faction who had planned to speak in front of the school board during public comments. This group of parents had known Mr. Jefferson from another school district, and they wanted to speak passionately on his behalf. Now these parents felt as though they had been denied this opportunity. They also felt as though the school board had colluded behind closed doors, choosing a candidate that suited their own needs instead of the needs of the students.

"I really don't see what the problem is," said the school board president. "You elected us to do a job, and we are doing that job. How it gets done should not bother you. In fact, we meet plenty of times without any public present just so we can get the work done."

Some of the parents complained in letters to the editor that the school board was not allowing community members to participate in legislative process regarding what happened in their schools. Not only were the community members excluded from having a voice to know what happened, but the school board effectively prevented media from attending meetings and reporting on the decisions that were made.

More and more, it seems like the school board operated as a clandestine good old boys' club.

A parent watch group filed a lawsuit against school board, claiming that because the board had met and acted in secrecy, their decision was not valid, and no superintendent had been chosen for the position.

When Jackie Black was told that her hiring was put on hold as a formality until the school board could meet in public with the community, she too filed a lawsuit against the members of the school board and the school district.

When the school board was finally able to meet at the public forum, more than 700 people had turned out for the meeting, including news reporters. The board room could hold only 100 or so people comfortably and safely, so cameras and TV screens had been set up to stream the meeting live to those people who had to watch from outside the building.

The first 15 minutes of meeting consisted of public comments, and many parents got up and spoke about which candidate they preferred for the position of superintendent of schools.

The members of the school board listened to the remarks and made their decision.

ISSUE

The Cypress Creek School District board has had a habit of meeting in secret. The school board members try to make the meeting dates and times convenient for themselves. Sometimes the superintendent's administrative assistant does not receive the agenda in time to post, or she forgets completely to make the public announcement regarding the upcoming meeting.

The school board met in secret, selected a candidate for the position of superintendent, and asked the candidate to write her own press release.

DILEMMA

When members of the community found out that they had been excluded from the process of selecting the new superintendent, they complained publicly, and a watchdog group filed a lawsuit against the school board members and the school district. The school board was forced to contact their choice for superintendent and tell her that they had to postpone the decision until they could have an unofficial and public meeting.

When she found out that her job was in jeopardy, the candidate for the superintendent position also filed a lawsuit against members of the school board and the school district.

Now the school board has to have a public meeting to make their decision.

QUESTIONS

1. Should the school board have met even though the notice was not posted?
2. What if four of the members had met informally off site to discuss their choice for new superintendent? Would that have been considered public or private meeting? Wouldn't that have been legal?
3. Should the school board continue with their decision to hire Jackie Black? Why or why not?
4. If you were Stewart Jefferson, would you withdraw your name from consideration? Why or why not?
5. What's wrong with the school board president saying that the school board members routinely meet without public notice?

Chapter 25

Supervision Saga

Urban School District
Standards: Professional Capacity of School Personnel, 6b c; Professional
  Community for Teachers and Staff, 7e

BACKGROUND

Paula Casa was named interim superintendent at the Moody Unified School District. Paula had originally been the director of curriculum and instruction, so it seemed like a natural progression to move into the superintendent role. At least that's how it seemed to Paula.

Paula had her eyes on the the Superintendent's job or a long time. She'd come from a family of educators. Both of her parents were teachers who had long since retired. Her brother Tim had taught math for a few years before becoming a finance officer. Her sister Agnes adored working with people, and she had gone into teaching, then social work, and then she became a human resources specialist.

It appeared as though education was in the Casas' blood.

Not everyone thought the Casas should be in education, however. Paula Casa was not the type of person you wanted to be upset with you. She tended to be vindictive, and she engaged in unethical behavior.

When she was a campus principal, Paula would routinely ask the consultant providing professional development for her teachers to leave the materials at school overnight if there was a multiple day training. When the consultant went back to his or her hotel, Paula had several of her employees photocopy all of the consultant's materials, so the campus would not have to purchase them. This way they could still use them after the consultant left, and their investment would be minimal.

When Paula became the assistant superintendent for curriculum and instruction, she brought some of her most trusted employees into central office with her, including her administrative assistant and her assistant principal. The administrative assistant continued to work side by side with her boss, and the assistant principal was promoted to a directorship.

Now that Paula Casa was the interim superintendent, she had more plans for filling positions in and around the district, and especially at central office.

At her first board meeting as the interim superintendent, Paula planned to recommend that her sister be hired to work in the human resources department. A position had just opened up, and even though it was not a supervisory position, Paula thought her sister could move into supervision within a year or two. All she had to do was get her sister into the department. Fortunately, Agnes had a different last name than her sister, so no one knew that Paula was intent on hiring a family member to fill the position.

The school board approved her recommendation.

Paula also wanted her brother to supervise the finances for the district. There was no one she trusted more for the job. When the job was posted, she encouraged her brother to apply for the position.

"Come on," she said. "You know you'll get the job, and I will make sure you get paid a lot of money. You haven't anything to lose."

Her brother interviewed for the position, and the interview committee selected him over the other candidates. Paula was relieved that she would not have to put down her superintendent's foot and force them to hire her brother.

Once again, in an executive session, Paula chose not to speak up and reveal the familial relationship she had with the school district's future finance assistant superintendent. Nonetheless, the school board went along with the committee's recommendation. Paula was silent.

Once her family members had been hired, Paula began to work on the line staff chart for the organization of the school district. This is the superintendent for finance reported to the superintendent, of course. That's the way it has always been, and Paula saw no reason to change that.

She did, however, want her sister to report to her. So she changed the title slightly, making Agnes the new HR confidant to the superintendent. She wrote up a job description and a rationale for why the superintendent of schools needed someone who would be a liaison between the human resources and the top leadership position in the district.

Again Paula took this request to the school board, where it was approved along with a host of other items in a single action one busy evening.

Paula smiled.

She had managed to get both her brother and sister hired, and no one knew that the three of them were related.

Paula's parents both worked as substitutes in the school district, however, and it wasn't long before her father mentioned in a teachers' lounge one day how proud he was of his three children.

"Oh, what districts do they work in?" asked a colleague who was also in the teachers' lounge.

Mr. Casa said, "Not districts. One district. This one!"

ISSUE

Paula Casa, the new superintendent, has hired her brother as the assistant superintendent for finance. She also hired her sister for a position at the district administration offices. Because Paula wants her family members reporting to her, she changed her sister's job title and description, as well as who her supervisor would be.

Although she had several opportunities to tell the school board about the family ties, Paula remained silent, allowing her family members to be hired and placed under her supervision.

DILEMMA

Paula's father, who frequently substituted at the schools in the district, revealed the family relationship while he was at one of the campuses.

The teacher he talked to posted the information on social media. It was not long before the news media picked up the story and publicized it even further.

As a result, parents, teachers, and community members began calling for the resignation of all three Casa family members: the human resource confidant, the assistant superintendent for finance, and the superintendent.

QUESTIONS

1. What responsibility does the superintendent have in making family relationships known?
2. Should a superintendent supervise a family member? Why or why not?

3. What's wrong with the superintendent changing the line and staff organization chart for the school district?
4. Is the employment of Paula's parents as substitute teachers in the same
   school district considered nepotism? Why or why not?
5. Should the school board continue Paula's employment as superintendent
   or broaden their search for another one? Explain your answer.

Chapter 26

Thrown Under the Bus

Suburban School District
Standards: Mission, Vision, and Core Values, 1d, e; School Improvement,
10a; Meaningful Engagement of Families and Community, 8a

BACKGROUND

Robin Roberts was not popular with the administrative leaders when she came to the Eastview School District, but she has been the school board's choice for filling the open position.

Many of the administrators had worked the district for a long time. They saw the new superintendent as a person who was meddling in their jobs. Superintendent Roberts always seemed to have a better way to do things, and they didn't like it. The cabinet members wanted to do business the way they have always done it. Now their new superintendent had new expectations of them.

The chief financial officer (CFO) of the district, Tracy Hayward, was especially unhappy with Superintendent Roberts. First of all, the new superintendent was one of those people who actually knew how to read a finance and loss statement. That was a huge problem for the CFO, because Tracy Hayward had been siphoning funds from a couple of accounts for the past nine years. It wasn't much money, just a little to see if it could be done. It turned out that it could, at least until Roberts arrived, and then she had to stop moving money into her account.

Hayward had also wanted to be the superintendent in Eastview, but she was not given the chance, thanks to the hiring of Roberts.

125

Hayward was, however, hoping to change that, and she had a plan. There were several other administrators in the cabinet who disliked their new boss; they had wanted Hayward to become the new superintendent. Together they collaborated on a plan to have the superintendent removed.

It began with small things. The special education director purposely did not attend an important meeting, and when she was asked about it by the school board, she said that the superintendent had never told her the date and time. The other administrators mentioned that they, too, had been left out of meetings. Clearly this was a sign that the superintendent was incompetent.

At school board meetings, the cabinet members in attendance purposely stated incorrect information that was not aligned to the information in the school board members' packets. When the school board members questioned the disparity, the administrators said that they had given the superintendent revised copies, and that they were apparently not included in the packet.

The various members of the cabinet and the other administrators in the district continued telling these lies and creating distortions. Each time, Superintendent Roberts disputed their claims, but it seemed like there were more people who believed her team rather than her.

"That's not true," she would say. "These are a bunch of lies."

When the superintendent finally confronted her cabinet team after several months of frustration, they offered excuses or simply said things like, "Don't you remember? I did bring it by. You must have forgotten. It happened, really it did. I left it right here. I can't believe you don't remember."

To make matters worse, when some of the central office administrators were out in the community, parents would ask questions about special education procedures or about the new reading program. "Oh, we can't talk about that," the administrators would say. "Superintendent's orders."

The parents were becoming increasingly frustrated with what was happening in the district.

At a town hall meeting with the superintendent and the cabinet, one parent stood up and announced loudly, "The problem here is that we got a failure to communicate. There are covert operations that are more transparent than what you've been doing. You are running the least transparent leadership program I've ever seen."

When Superintendent Roberts asked what he meant, the man turned away in disgust.

She walked over to the microphone: "Look, I don't know what's going on here, but I'd like to get to the bottom of this."

"Is that a threat?" asked a parent.

"No," said the superintendent. "It's not a threat at all. I'd genuinely like to find out why you don't seem to able to trust me."

"You don't trust your people," said a third parent. "You got good people working for you, and you are throwing them under the bus. Making them look bad."

"Throwing them under the bus?" exclaimed the superintendent. "I don't think so."

Superintendent Roberts knew she had to get a handle on the situation. It had gotten completely out of control. When she returned to her office, she had a message to call the school board president.

She dialed the phone.

The board president said, "Tracy Hayward just called me. She tells me she suspects that someone has been misappropriating funds. Using district money and equipment for personal use."

"What?" cried the superintendent. "I see those finance spreadsheets and statements every month. There's no way."

"I was afraid of that," said the school board president. "She thinks it's you, Robin."

ISSUE

The administrators in Eastview District are colluding against the current superintendent. They are doing everything they can to make the superintendent seem incapable of doing her job. They make her seem forgetful and incompetent, when in fact the superintendent is none of these things.

The CFO is behind this effort because she wanted to be the new superintendent and was not even interviewed for the position.

It has come to the school board president's attention that more troubles have surfaced. The CFO called him with an accusation that the new superintendent has been misappropriating funds. Because the superintendent would have seen something like that in a budget sheet—and did not report it—the board president thinks the accusation may have some validity.

DILEMMA

Some of the administrators in the district have distorted the truth so badly regarding the superintendent's leadership that even the parents in the community have stopped believing or trusting the superintendent.

Every time the superintendent confronted these employees, they had a backup or an alibi. Sometimes they blatantly lied about a situation, but the superintendent had not been able to catch them in the lie.

Even the parents have become frustrated, aiming their anger at the superintendent.

Now the school board president is suspicious that the superintendent may have used district funds for personal use.

Robin Roberts said, "They threw me under the bus."

QUESTIONS

1. How should a superintendent help employees adapt to inevitable change?
2. How could the superintendent be sure that employees get proper notice of meetings?
3. What mistake did the superintendent make in addressing the employee lies? What should she have done instead?
4. At what point should the superintendent have involved the school board? Why?
5. If you were the superintendent, what would be your next steps and why?

Chapter 27

How We've Always Done It

Rural District
Standards: Mission, Vision, and Core Values, 1c; Equity and Cultural Responsiveness, 3a, b

BACKGROUND

The Dwainville Independent School District (ISD) used to be a tiny community inconveniently located in the middle of nowhere. The rural district was the biggest employer in the area, and not only did everyone know everyone else, but they also called each other by their first names, regardless of job title.

Most of the residents grew up together, and families helped each other out. They spent leisure time together, too, fishing in the nearby river or hunting in the fall. They had cookouts, high school football, and good memories of growing up in Dwainville.

As some of the older family matriarchs and patriarchs passed on, however, Dwainville began to change. It was gradual at first, but then the changes became more pronounced. The town added a grocery store, a couple of fast-food restaurants, several stop lights, and there was talk of a Walmart store coming in, too.

Many of the adult children in these families, however, had sought jobs in urban areas. The population growth in Dwainville was the result of city people wanting to adopt what they thought would be a more idyllic lifestyle. The large parcels of land were subdivided, and neighborhoods took root where once crops stood in the fields and cattle grazed in pastures. The biggest neighborhood already had over 5,000 homes in it. More were being planned and built.

These new families brought more than just their children with them. They also brought diversity, and that was something Dwainville had little experience with.

Already the district was shocked by the realization that subpopulation performance on standardized assessments could come back to bite them.

In the past, Dwainville ISD had no subpopulations to speak of. At least 99% of the students were Caucasian. Less than 1% were identified for special education services. There were two bilingual children in the elementary school, but the school decided to immerse them in English since they weren't required to provide bilingual education services.

Table 27.1 Progress Results for Dwainville Independent School District

Indicator: Achievement on State Assessment Performance and CCR Readiness	Percentage Passing
Overall student performance	81
Economically disadvantaged student performance	26
English language learner student performance	37
Special education student performance	19

Dwainville, with a current enrollment of approximately 3,000 students, always maintained that its students were far more than a number or a score on an achievement test. Their students were multifaceted individuals with plenty of interests and options.

The district offered a robust extracurricular program for students, and in the past, it was well attended. The activities consisted of two categories: sports and Future Farmers of America, and most students participated in something. Some of the students participated in several activities.

Table 27.2 Student Activity Participation

Activity	Elementary School: No. of Students Participating	Middle School: No. of Students Participating	High School: No. of Students Participating
Football	0	37	78
Baseball	0	21	32
Basketball	0	16	20
Cheerleading	14	15	40
Band	0	26	113
Volleyball	0	12	11
Softball	0	14	23
FFA	11	8	55
Rodeo Club	2	21	39
Outdoor Adventurers Club	0	0	17
Fellowship of Christian Athletes	0	0	6

Some of the other issues about diversity weren't measurable on student achievement tests, but the differences were apparent, nonetheless. Dwainville ISD was once a Christian community, where faith in God and community prayer were important. Now, approximately 5% of the community was atheistic or agnostic. Another 15% associated themselves with religions other than Christianity.

Superintendent Ricky Meyers had to admit it. Dwainville had changed.

He hoped it was for the better.

ISSUE

There had been rumblings over the past eighteen months that the new parents, of whom there were many, were unhappy with the school district and with the administration. The parents felt as though their children's needs weren't being met.

At the beginning of this school year, they had asked for a variety of new extracurricular activities. Their children wanted to play soccer and start a technology club. They wanted to create a Go Green Initiative and a drama group, and they wanted to express themselves and their interests in the activities.

The administration turned down every request, insisting that Dwainville ISD offered plenty of diverse activities already. The students could choose from one of those, they said.

Clearly, the administration hadn't been listening. They continued doing business how they had always done it.

DILEMMA

Now a group of parents are demanding to see Superintendent Ricky Meyers. They are frustrated that their children cannot be involved in activities that interest them.

"Not everyone likes football, and not everyone is a cowboy," said one of the parents. Those gathered around her murmured their agreement. "Our children have a right to have their cultural interests and needs met."

"Ma'am, we're doing the best we can. This is what we offer. Take it or leave it," said the superintendent.

A single figure dressed in a suit and tie emerged from the throng. "No," he said. "I don't think that's how it's going to work out at all." The man handed Ricky Meyers his business card. "You see," said the man, "I want to talk with you about how you're denying the children of these taxpayers their rights. We also need to talk about that prayer thing in your school meetings. The AFL-CIO believes you've violated our Resolution 44."

QUESTIONS

1. Why doesn't the Dwainville Elementary School have to provide bilingual education to the two students they have? Should they offer bilingual education anyway?
2. The statement assessment scores reveal a large gap between what could be called Dwainville's former population and the students currently enrolled in the DISD schools. What is the cause of the disparity?
3. The second data set is for student participation in extracurricular activities. What do the enrollment numbers show?
4. How would you advise the superintendent to handle his inevitable conversation with the AFL-CIO representative?
5. How could this scenario have been avoided?

Bibliography

Ackerman, Dave. (n.d.). *Superintendent Sharing*. Central Lyon CSD. Retrieved from http://www.centrallyon.org/vnews/display.v/ART/4886a5051fd88

Anonymous. (April 9, 2014). *"Pay-to-Play" at Schools Has Some Crying "Foul!"* Lawyers.com. Retrieved from http://education-law.lawyers.com/school-law/pay-to-play-at-schools-has-some-crying-foul.html

Barber, Mark. (February 21, 2017). *New CMS Superintendent Addresses Challenges Facing School District*. WSOCTV. Retrieved from http://www.wsoctv.com/news/local/new-cms-superintendent-addresses-challenges-facing-school-district/496080685

Bies, Jessica. (February 13, 2014). *UPDATED: Waseca Superintendent and Legal Aid Organization Paint Different Pictures of School Lunch Program*. Southernminn.com. Retrieved from http://www.southernminn.com/waseca_county_news/news/article_d0e50017-1747-5e27-b86f-671e58e67cd4.html

Bisson, David. (January 10, 2017). *Ransomware Attack Leads LA School to Fork Over $28K in Ransom*. Tripwire, Inc. Retrieved from https://www.tripwire.com/state-of-security/latest-security-news/ransomware-attack-leads-la-school-fork-28k-ransom/

Brookings.edu. (n.d.). *Education Choice and Competition Index*. Brookings. edu. Retrieved from https://www.brookings.edu/wp-content/uploads/2017/03/ccf_20170329_ecci_scoring_guide_summary.pdf

Bulman, May. (April 15, 2017). *Schools May Shut Down Next Term as Teachers Vote to Strike Over Cash Crisis*. The Independent. Retrieved from http://www.independent.co.uk/news/education/education-news/schools-close-strike-action-teachers-nut-conference-summer-a7685376.html

Callahan, John. (January 11, 2014). *Schools Defend Their Class-Size Violations*. Ocala. Retrieved from http://www.ocala.com/article/LK/20140112/News/604137072/OS/

Cambridge Public Schools. (April 14, 2016). *Assistant Superintendent for Curriculum & Instruction*. Top School Jobs. Retrieved from http://www.topschooljobs.org/JobSeekerX/ViewJobRSS.asp?cjid=207464&AccountNo=2202

Chambers, Jennifer. (September 13, 2016). *Suit: Detroit School Children Denied Right to Literacy. Detroit News.* Retrieved from http://www.detroitnews.com/story/news/local/detroit-city/2016/09/13/lawsuit-detroit-schoolchildren-literacy/90298836/

Chandler, D. L. (May 13, 2017*). Bullying Video Surfaces of 8-Year-Old Boy Who Committed Suicide.* Yahoo! Beauty. Retrieved from https://www.yahoo.com/beauty/bullying-video-surfaces-8-year-old-boy-committed-suicide-201134655.html

Charters, Justen. (May 13, 2017). *Parents Sound Alarms Over Teenage Suicide Ritual Called "The Blue Whale Challenge."* Independent Journal Review. Retrieved from http://ijr.com/2017/05/871698-parents-sound-alarms-teenage-suicide-ritual-called-blue-whale-challenge/

Chiaramonte, Perry. (June 6, 2017). *Pennsylvania School District Hit with "Ghost Teacher"; Lawsuit.* Fox News Network. Retrieved from http://www.foxnews.com/us/2017/06/06/pennsylvania-school-district-hit-with-ghost-teacher-lawsuit.html

Chipp, Timothy. (May 3, 2017). *UPDATE: Texas Teacher Evaluation Lawsuit Settled.* Abilene Reporter-News. Retrieved from http://www.reporternews.com/story/news/education/2017/05/03/texas-teacher-evaluation-lawsuit-settled/101267090/

Cornwell, Paige. (February 17, 2017). *King County Judge Rules State's Charter-School Law Is Constitutional. The Seattle Times.* Retrieved from http://www.seattletimes.com/seattle-news/education/king-county-judge-rules-states-charter-school-law-is-constitutional/

Crime Sider Staff. (March 14, 2017). *Haeli Wey, Ex-Teacher, Gets Probation after Admitting Relationships with Students.* CBS News. Retrieved from http://www.cbsnews.com/news/haeli-wey-ex-teacher-gets-probation-after-admitting-relationships-with-students/

Crime Sider Staff. (n.d.). *Notorious Teacher Sex Scandals.* CBS News. Retrieved from http://www.cbsnews.com/pictures/notorious-teacher-sex-scandals/8/

Dart, Kaitlyn. (n.d.). *Removal of Superintendent: New Start.* Move On. Retrieved from http://petitions.moveon.org/sign/removal-of-superintendent-2

Dorigo Jones, Bobby. (February 13, 2017). *Askwith Essentials—Driving Change: The Challenges Superintendents Face in Urban Schools.* Harvard. Retrieved from https://www.gse.harvard.edu/news/17/02/askwith-essentials-driving-change-challenges-superintendents-face-urban-schools

Dungca, Nicole. (February 14, 2014). *Portland Teachers Strike: Leaders Cautiously Optimistic, Workload and Salary among Key Unresolved Issues.* OregonLive. Retrieved from http://www.oregonlive.com/portland/index.ssf/2014/02/portland_teachers_strike_leade.html

Fensterwald, John. (n.d.). *Students Matter Sues Districts over Teacher Evaluations.* EdSource. Retrieved from https://edsource.org/2015/students-matter-sues-districts-over-teacher-evaluations/83103

Friedersdorf, Conor. (June 29, 2014). *Firing Bad Teachers: A Superintendent and a Teacher's Union Official Debate. The Atlantic.* Retrieved from https://www.theatlantic.com/education/archive/2014/06/firing-bad-teachers-a-superintendent-and-a-teachers-union-official-debate/373651/

Gallagher, Shannon. (February 20, 2017). *SWAT Team Assists in School Active Shooter Drills. Wicked Local.* Retrieved from http://brockton.wickedlocal.com/news/20170220/swat-team-assists-in-school-active-shooter-drills

Geuss, Megan. (February 21, 2015). *After iPad Initiative Failure, School Supe Says LA Can't Buy Computers for All. Ars Technica.* Retrieved from https://arstechnica.com/information-technology/2015/02/after-ipad-initiative-failure-school-supe-says-la-cant-buy-computers-for-all/

Gonzalez, Charles. (March 31, 2017). *Former Seguin ISD Superintendent Faced Sexual Harassment Claim before Resignation.* KSAT. Retrieved from http://www.ksat.com/news/defenders/former-seguin-isd-superintendent-faced-sexual-harassment-claim-before-resignation

Green, E. L. (January 20, 2017). *Howard County Officials Call Legal Dispute between Superintendent and School Board a Troubling Distraction. Baltimore Sun.* Retrieved from http://www.baltimoresun.com/news/maryland/bs-md-ho-foose-lawsuit-folo-20170120-story.html

Green, Erica. (January 20, 2017). *Howard County Officials Call Legal Dispute between Superintendent and School Board a Troubling Distraction. Baltimore Sun.* Retrieved from http://www.baltimoresun.com/news/maryland/bs-md-ho-foose-lawsuit-folo-20170120-story.html

Grey, Bernadette. (December 21, 2016). *What to Remember When Negotiating a Teachers Union Contract.* School Leaders Now. Retrieved from https://schoolleadersnow.weareteachers.com/frustrations-teachers-union-contract-negotiation/

Hanlon, Tegan. (May 12, 2017). *Waiting on Lawmakers, Anchorage School District Will Send Layoff Notices to 200 Teachers. Alaska Dispatch News.* Retrieved from https://www.adn.com/alaska-news/2017/05/12/anchorage-school-district-will-lay-off-about-200-teachers-in-face-of-budget-uncertainty/

Hargrove, Dorian. (March 3, 2017). *San Ysidro School District Supe Sued. San Diego Reader.* Retrieved from http://www.sandiegoreader.com/news/2017/mar/03/ticker-san-ysidro-school-district-supe-sued/

House, Samantha. (June 7, 2017). *Vandals Deflated Skaneateles School Bus Tires on Seniors' Last Day of High School.* Syracuse. Retrieved from http://www.syracuse.com/crime/index.ssf/2017/06/vandals_deflated_skaneateles_school_bus_tires_on_seniors_last_day_of_high_school.html

Jankowski, Stephanie. (May 23, 2017). *When Things Fall Apart: The Abuse of School-Board Power.* WeAreTeachers. Retrieved from https://www.weareteachers.com/when-things-fall-apart-the-abuse-of-school-board-power/

Jones, Chris. (n.d.). *Tooele School Superintendent Defends Questionable Degree.* KUTV. Retrieved from http://kutv.com/news/local/tooele-school-superintendent-says-he-did-not-lie-about-degree

Kadvany, E. (January 23, 2016). *Supe: Palo Alto School District Not Informed by Principal about Sex-Abuse Investigation.* Palo Alto Online. Retrieved from https://www.paloaltoonline.com/news/2016/01/22/superintendent-district-not-informed-about-sex-abuse-investigation

Kastner, Lindsay. (April 21, 2013). *New School a Major Change for Charter District.* My San Antonio. Retrieved from http://www.mysanantonio.com/news/education/article/New-school-a-major-change-for-charter-district-4450488.php

Kenrick, Chris. (February 8, 2013). *Feds: School District Violated Student's Civil Rights.* Palo Alto Online. Retrieved from https://www.paloaltoonline.com/news/2013/02/08/feds-school-district-violated-students-civil-rights

Leads, Chris. (June 7, 2017). *Public Seeks Schools Superintendent "Immediate" Removal; Caulfield "Sick of the Misinformation."* TAPinto. Retrieved from https://www.tapinto.net/towns/flemington-slash-raritan/articles/public-seeks-schools-superintendent-immediate-r

Leal, Fermi. (n.d.). *California Teachers Get Layoff Notices Despite Teacher Shortages.* EdSource. Retrieved from https://edsource.org/2017/california-teachers-get-layoff-notices-despite-teacher-shortages/578675

Lipovich, Joe. (May 8, 2017). *Blue Whale Challenge: Danbury Superintendent Warns of Dangerous Social Media Trend.* Patch. Retrieved from https://patch.com/connecticut/danbury/blue-whale-challenge-danbury-superintendent-warns-dangerous-social-media-trend

Luryer, Rebecca. (n.d.). *Superintendent Moss "Unintentionally" Guilty, Fined as Part of Deal to Avoid Ethics Hearing.* Island Packet. Retrieved from http://www.islandpacket.com/news/local/community/beaufort-news/article94856127.html

Martire, Ralph. (February 5, 2016). *Lack of Money Is the Root of Problems for CPS Schools.* Daily Herald. Retrieved from http://www.dailyherald.com/article/20160205/discuss/160209402/

Miller, Thaddeus. (February 4, 2017). *Livingston Schools, Police Train for a Mass Shooting on Campus.* Merced Sun-Star. Retrieved from http://www.mercedsunstar.com/news/local/community/livingston/article130819739.html

Nadworny, Elissa. (November 4, 2016). *Middle School Suicides Reach an All-Time High.* NPR. Retrieved from http://www.npr.org/sections/ed/2016/11/04/500659746/middle-school-suicides-reach-an-all-time-high

Nati, Michelle. (April 29, 2014). *8 Unbelievable Twitter Public Relations Disasters (Twitter, Campaign, Viral, Failure).* ODDEE. Retrieved from http://www.oddee.com/item_98944.aspx

National Policy Board for Educational Administration. (2015). Professional Standards for Educational Leaders 2015. Reston, VA: Author. Retrieved from http://npbea.org/wp-content/uploads/2017/06/Professional-Standards-for-Educational-Leaders_2015.pdf

Nesbit, Jeff. (May 6, 2015). *Institutional Racism Is Our Way of Life.* U.S. News & World Report. Retrieved from https://www.usnews.com/news/blogs/at-the-edge/2015/05/06/institutional-racism-is-our-way-of-life

NO AUTHOR. (March 16, 2015). *FCPS Superintendent Found in Violation of Hiring Practices.* The State Journal. Retrieved from http://www.state-journal.com/2015/03/16/fcps-superintendent-found-in-violation-of-hiring-practices/

NO AUTHOR. (July 7, 2015). *Bullying and Suicide.* Bullying Statistics. Retrieved from http://www.bullyingstatistics.org/content/bullying-and-suicide.html

NO AUTHOR. (July 29, 2015). *State Laws Ban Access to Workers' Social Media Accounts.* SHRM. Retrieved from https://www.shrm.org/resourcesandtools/legal-and-compliance/state-and-local-updates/pages/states-social-media.aspx

NO AUTHOR. (January 19, 2016). *The Out-of-District Charter School Scam Has Landed One CA Supe a Felony Charge: Take Heed Randy Dorn.* Seattle Education. Retrieved from https://seattleeducation2010.wordpress.com/2016/01/19/the-out-of-district-charter-school-scam-has-landed-one-ca-supe-a-felony-charge-take-heed-randy-dorn/

NO AUTHOR. (May 25, 2016). *Candidate Arrested, Carried Out of Brevard School Board Meeting after Saying "penis."* WFTV. Retrieved from http://www.wftv. com/news/local/candidate-arrested-carried-out-of-brevard-school-board-meeting-after-saying-penis/302445490

NO AUTHOR. (September 7, 2016). *Yuba City Teacher: Strike Is "Only Option We Have Left."* Retrieved from http://www.kcra.com/article/yuba-city-teacher-strike-is-only-option-we-have-left/6430448

NO AUTHOR. (November 16, 2016). *Accusations of North Murray Teacher Taking Inappropriate Pictures of Female Student.* News 12 Now. Retrieved from http://wdef.com/2016/11/16/accusations-north-murray-teacher-taking-inappropriate-pictures-female-student/

NO AUTHOR. (December 19, 2016). *Baton Rouge Shooting: 3 Police Dead & 3 Injured, Shooter Dead—LA Superintendent.* RT.com. Retrieved from https://www.rt.com/usa/351706-baton-rouge-cops-shot/

NO AUTHOR. (December 21, 2016). *What to Remember When Negotiating a Teachers Union Contract—School Leaders Now.* Retrieved from https://schoolleaders now.weareteachers.com/frustrations-teachers-union-contract-negotiation/

NO AUTHOR. (February 21, 2017). *New CMS Superintendent Addresses Challenges Facing School District.* WSOC-TV. Retrieved from http://www.wsoctv. com/news/local/new-cms-superintendent-addresses-challenges-facing-school-district/496080685

NO AUTHOR. (April 10, 2017). *San Bernardino Elementary School Shooting: Teacher, 8-Year-Old Student Killed in Murder-Suicide.* Fox News. Retrieved from http://www.foxnews.com/us/2017/04/10/san-bernardino-elementary-school-shooting-2-reported-dead-in-suspected-murder-suicide.html

NO AUTHOR. (April 13, 2017). *Blanco ISD Board to Eye Suspension of Counselor Accused of Improper Relationship. DailyTrib.com—Your Hill Country Online News Authority.* Retrieved from http://www.dailytrib.com/2017/04/13/blanco-isd-board-eye-suspension-teacher-accused-improper-relationship/

NO AUTHOR. (May 1, 2017). *Huntsville City Schools Superintendent Says Changes Could Be Coming to Behavioral Learning Guide.* WHNT. Retrieved from http://whnt.com/2017/05/01/huntsville-city-schools-superintendent-says-changes-could-be-coming-to-behavioral-learning-guide/

NO AUTHOR. (May 15, 2017). *Well-Paid Florida Superintendent Gets 8-Figure Payout Despite Sexual Harassment Accusations.* EAGnews. Retrieved from http://eagnews.org/well-paid-florida-superintendent-gets-8-figure-payout-despite-sexual-harassment-accusations/

NO AUTHOR. (May 24, 2017). *Deputy: 1 Ejected, Several Injured in School Bus vs. Dump Truck Crash.* WISC. Retrieved from http://www.channel3000.com/news/crews-respond-to-school-bus-crash-in-grant-county/513313968

NO AUTHOR. (n.d). *AASA | American Association of School Administrators.* Retrieved from http://www.aasa.org/SchoolAdministratorArticle.aspx?id=10062

NO AUTHOR. (n.d). *Askwith Essentials—Driving Change: The Challenges Superintendents Face in Urban Schools.* Harvard Graduate School of Education. Retrieved from https://www.gse.harvard.edu/news/17/02/askwith-essentials-driving-change-challenges-superintendents-face-urban-schools

NO AUTHOR. (n.d.). *Dr. Smith: Resign as MCPS Superintendent*. Change.org. Retrieved from https://www.change.org/p/dr-smith-resign-as-mcps-superintendent

NO AUTHOR. (n.d.). *Five Principles to Protect Student Data Privacy*. Parent Coalition for Student Privacy. Retrieved from https://www.studentprivacymatters.org/five-principles-to-protect-student-data-privacy/

NO AUTHOR. (n.d.). *I'm a Teacher, and I Know IEPs Aren't Being Followed. What Do I Do?* The Wrightslaw Way. Retrieved from http://www.wrightslaw.com/blog/im-a-teacher-and-i-know-ieps-arent-being-followed-what-do-i-do/

NO AUTHOR. (n.d.). Job. *View Job*. Retrieved from http://www.topschooljobs.org/JobSeekerX/ViewJobRSS.asp?cjid=207464&AccountNo=2202

NO AUTHOR. (n.d.). *Louisville Superintendent: Teachers Might Have Deleted Files before Strike—News—Columbus Monthly—Columbus, OH*. Retrieved from http://www.columbusmonthly.com/news/20161123/louisville-superintendent-teachers-might-have-deleted-files-before-strike

NO AUTHOR. (n.d.). *Managing Teacher Layoffs | Tips for Surviving Downsizing*. AllEducationSchools.com. Retrieved from http://www.alleducationschools.com/secondary-education/teacher-layoffs/

NO AUTHOR. (n.d.). *MoveOn Petitions—Removal of Superintendent: New Start*. Retrieved from http://petitions.moveon.org/sign/removal-of-superintendent-2

NO AUTHOR. (n.d.). *Password Protected: States Pass Anti-Snooping Laws*. The Pew Charitable Trusts. Retrieved from http://www.pewtrusts.org/en/research-and-analysis/blogs/stateline/2014/07/08/password-protected-states-pass-anti-snooping-laws

NO AUTHOR. (n.d.). *Petition·Dr. Smith: Resign as MCPS Superintendent·Change.org*. Retrieved from https://www.change.org/p/dr-smith-resign-as-mcps-superintendent

NO AUTHOR. (n.d.). *ScholarWorks @ Georgia State University*. Site. Retrieved from http://scholarworks.gsu.edu/eps_facpub/25/

NO AUTHOR. (n.d.). *School Board Basics—How Schools Are Run*. Retrieved from http://www.oldbridgeadmin.org/board_education.cfm?subpage=1149520

NO AUTHOR. (n.d.). *School Board Recalls*. Ballotpedia. Retrieved from https://ballotpedia.org/School_board_recalls

NO AUTHOR. (n.d.). *School Safety during Emergencies: What Parents Need to Know*. HealthyChildren.org. Retrieved from https://www.healthychildren.org/English/safety-prevention/all-around/Pages/Actions-Schools-Are-Taking-to-Make-Themselves-Safer.aspx

NO AUTHOR. (n.d.). *School Safety/Emergency Response Procedures*. VALLEY VIEW 365U. Retrieved from https://www.vvsd.org/Page/129

NO AUTHOR. (n.d.). *Security Breach Steals Tax Info for All Bloomington Public School Employees. Star Tribune*. Retrieved from http://www.startribune.com/security-breach-steals-tax-info-for-all-bloomington-public-school-employees/413632393/

NO AUTHOR. (n.d.). *Supe Deserves No Credit for Pay to Play Progress*. Thousand Oaks Acorn. Retrieved from http://www.toacorn.com/news/2017-05-04/Letters/Supe_deserves_no_credit_for_pay_to_play_progress.html

NO AUTHOR. (n.d.). *What to Do—Bomb Threat*. Homeland Security. Retrieved from https://www.dhs.gov/what-to-do-bomb-threat

NO AUTHOR. (n.d.). *News*. Retrieved from http://www.seacoastecho.com/article_ 10648.shtml#.WSgoSbzyu8U

NO AUTHOR. (n.d.). *San Ysidro School Superintendent Hired Girlfriend, Fired Whistleblower*. San Diego's Original Latino Community Newspaper. Retrieved from http://laprensa-sandiego.org/breaking-news/san-ysidro-school-superintendent-covered-up-hiring-female-companion/

Ojeda, Sofia. (August 7, 2015). *Thousands of Katy ISD Employees' Info Potentially Leaked in IRS Audit*. KPRC. Retrieved from http://www.click2houston.com/news/ thousands-of-katy-isd-employees-info-potentially-leaked-in-irs-audit

Old Bridge Township Public Schools. (n.d.). *School Board Basics*. Old Bridge Township Public Schools. Retrieved from http://www.oldbridgeadmin.org/board_educa tion.cfm?subpage=1149520

Paul, Joeseph. (May 1, 2017). *North Newton Superintendent Arrested for OWI*. *Journal & Courier*. Retrieved from http://www.jconline.com/story/news/ crime/2017/05/01/north-newton-superintendent-arrested-owi/101157668/

Peguero, Joshua. (May 16, 2017*). Brookesmith ISD Superintendent Says School Will Be Open Next Year*. KTXS. Retrieved from http://www.ktxs.com/news/ brookesmith-isd-superintendent-says-school-will-be-open-next-year/501916000

Prosise/Himes, Roger/Lynn. (n.d.). *The Collective Bargaining Tightrope*. AASA. Retrieved from http://www.aasa.org/SchoolAdministratorArticle.aspx?id=10062

Riddell, Roger. (June 8, 2017). *Can Sharing Superintendents Improve Education across Small Districts?* Education Dive. Retrieved from http://www.educationdive.com/ news/can-sharing-superintendents-improve-education-across-small-districts/444481/

Ruggiero, Angela. (March 18, 2017). *Fired Pleasanton School Superintendent Accused of Sexual Harassment*. *East Bay Times*. Retrieved from http://www. eastbaytimes.com/2017/03/18/fired-pleasanton-school-superintendent-accused-of-sexual-harassment/

San Diegans for Open Government. (April 27, 2017). *SDOG Sues Poway Unified School District, Three Board Members for Open-Meeting Violations in Hiring New Superintendent*. Sandiegans4opengov. Retrieved from https://sandiegans4opengov. wordpress.com/2017/04/27/sdog-sues-poway-unified-school-district-board-mem bers-for-open-meeting-violations-in-hiring-new-superintendent/

Seidel, Aly. (July 7, 2014). *What We Don't Know about Summer School*. NPR. Retrieved from http://www.npr.org/sections/ed/2014/07/07/323659124/ what-we-dont-know-about-summer-school

Shamsian, Jacob. (December 6, 2015). *One Company Is Teaching Schools How to Deal with Active Shooters—And It's Making Teachers Uncomfortable. Business Insider*. Retrieved from http://www.businessinsider.com/teachers-students-alice-fight-defend-school-mass-shooters

Sheridan, Lorna. (June 6, 2017). *Louann Carlomagno Resigns*. Sonoma Index Tribune. Retrieved from http://www.sonomanews.com/news/7071919-181/schools-superintendent-carlomagno-resigns?artslide=0 1

Silverman, Ellie. (November 12, 2016). *Special-ed Student Confined 617 Times in 6 Months Despite State Laws. The Seattle Times*. Retrieved from http://www.seat tletimes.com/seattle-news/education/special-ed-student-confined-617-times-in-6-months-despite-state-laws/

Singleton-Rickman, Lisa. (April 3, 2016). *Ethics Complaint Filed against Superintendent*. *Timesdaily*. Retrieved from http://www.timesdaily.com/news/education/ethics-complaint-filed-against-superintendent/article_884f8dba-64c6-51eb-b8bc-b70fabbe0410.html

Soave, R. (January 15, 2017). *A School Administrator Corrected a Student's Spelling on Twitter. She Was Fired*. Reason.com. Retrieved from http://reason.com/blog/2017/01/15/a-school-administrator-corrected-a-stude

Spencer, Jack. (n.d.). *Dealing with Dirty Bombs: Plain Facts, Practical Solutions*. The Heritage Foundation. Retrieved from http://www.heritage.org/homeland-security/report/dealing-dirty-bombs-plain-facts-practical-solutions

Stewart, Scott. (May 11, 2017). *Embattled Superintendent of Treynor Community School District Will Step Down This Summer*. Omaha. Retrieved from http://www.omaha.com/news/education/embattled-superintendent-of-treynor-community-school-district-will-step-down/article_ec8ee894-d092-514a-94d6-ca6c8fb1c353.html

Strauss, Valerie. (April 1, 2015). *How and Why Convicted Atlanta Teachers Cheated on Standardized Tests*. *Washington Post*. Retrieved from https://www.washingtonpost.com/news/answer-sheet/wp/2015/04/01/how-and-why-convicted-atlanta-teachers-cheated-on-standardized-tests/?utm_term=.cb0ea1bacca5

Strauss, Valerie. (November 12, 2015). *The Astonishing Amount of Data Being Collected about Your Children*. WP Company. Retrieved from https://www.washingtonpost.com/news/answer-sheet/wp/2015/11/12/the-astonishing-amount-of-data-being-collected-about-your-children/?utm_term=.53ad0d02ce2e

Strauss, Valerie. (March 30, 2017). *DeVos Criticized Denver for Its School Choice Policies. Now Denver's Superintendent Fires Back*. *Washington Post*. Retrieved from https://www.washingtonpost.com/news/answer-sheet/wp/2017/03/30/devos-criticized-denver-for-its-school-choice-policies-now-denvers-superintendent-fires-back/?utm_term=.1062b6b6d784

Strauss, Valerie. (April 29, 2017). *Schools Superintendent: Students Are Harming Themselves and Citing "13 Reasons Why."* *The Washington Post*. Retrieved from https://www.washingtonpost.com/news/answer-sheet/wp/2017/04/29/school-superintendent-students-are-harming-themselves-and-citing-13-reasons-why/?utm_term=.a446ebf3e428

Sturtz, Ken. (April 15, 2016). *Central Square Superintendent, Arrested for Drunken Driving, Suspended by Board*. Syracuse. Retrieved from http://www.syracuse.com/news/index.ssf/2016/04/central_square_superintendent_joseph_a_menard.html

Swinney, Connie. (April 13, 2017). *Blanco ISD Board to Eye Suspension of Counselor Accused of Improper Relationship*. *Daily Trib*. Retrieved from http://www.dailytrib.com/2017/04/13/blanco-isd-board-eye-suspension-teacher-accused-improper-relationship/

Trotter, Greg. (February 16, 2015). *Husband of District 113's Next Superintendent Accused of Online Bullying*. Highland Park News. Retrieved from http://www.chicagotribune.com/suburbs/highland-park/news/ct-hpn-highland-park-superintendent-husband-tl-20150216-story.html

Tsai, Joyce. (September 21, 2016). *Judge Rules against Requiring Standard-ized Test Scores in East Bay Teacher Evaluations. East Bay Times*. Retrieved from http://www.eastbaytimes.com/2016/09/20/judge-rules-against-requiring-standardized-test-scores-in-teacher-evaluations/

Vaznis, James. (October 2, 2010). *Boston Schools Violated Rights*. Boston. Retrieved from http://archive.boston.com/news/local/massachusetts/articles/2010/10/02/boston_schools_violated_rights/

Wall, Karen. (June 26, 2015). *Resident Accuses School Board Member of Ethics Violation*. Brick, NJ Patch. Retrieved from https://patch.com/new-jersey/brick/resident-accuses-school-board-member-ethics-violation-0

WBTV Web Staff. (November 28, 2016). *School Board Member, Woman Charged with Trafficking Meth in Lancaster*. WBTV. Retrieved from http://www.wbtv.com/story/33809268/school-board-member-woman-charged-with-trafficking-meth-in-lancaster

Weir, Kelli. (November 23, 2016). *Louisville Superintendent: Teachers Might Have Deleted Files before Strike. Columbus Monthly*. Retrieved from http://www.columbusmonthly.com/news/20161123/louisville-superintendent-teachers-might-have-deleted-files-before-strike

WTVC. (n.d.). *"Our Hearts Are Broken:" Superintendent Holds News Conference on School Bus Tragedy*. WTVC. Retrieved from http://newschannel9.com/news/local/superintendent-holds-news-conference-on-school-bus-tragedy

About the Author

Dr. Wafa Hozien's professional background includes over 20 years' work as a high school history teacher and school administrator. Dr. Hozien has designed and delivered training for school districts, universities, and leadership academies throughout the United States and internationally. She specializes in combining research-based strategies and practical applications, working with school administrators, teacher leaders, and school districts to adopt innovative strategies for their locations. Specifically, the incorporation of issues related to culture, ethnicity, race, and religion in the education process is valued by Dr. Hozien as integral and important.

Dr. Hozien has published numerous articles and publications on diversity issues in education. To help reduce inequities in education, Dr. Hozien makes herself available by educating through interactive workshops at schools, community organizations, and campus lectures on cultural competency and social justice. She has been researching adolescent minority female public schooling experiences. In the multicultural education context, she has published and presented at workshops and conferences on minority student experiences.

Presently, she teaches graduate students in the United States in principal/superintendent doctoral preparation programs. Nondiscrimination and equality are key principles that Dr. Hozien applies to education in all of the courses she teaches.

Dr. Hozien appreciates constructive feedback and gaining insight as to best practices and ways to improve this book. If you find that this book is missing something or have suggestions for improvement, kindly contact the author via e-mail. Dr. Hozien can be reached at whozien@gmail.com.

Dr. Hozien's most recent book is entitled SLLA Crash Course: Approaches for Success (2017). New York: Rowman and Littlefield.

Made in the
USA
Middletown, DE